PASSING ON
THE BATON

JOHN W. McELROY

Passing On the Baton

ISBN-13: 978-1-886296-42-8
ISBN-10: 1-886296-42-1

Arrow Publications
P.O. Box 10102
Cedar Rapids, IA 52410
Phone: (319) 395-7833
Toll Free: (877) 363-6889 (U.S. only)
Fax: (319) 395-7353
Web: www.arrowbookstore.com

Additional copies of Passing On the Baton can be ordered through the Churchlands website: www.churchlands.org.au or by phone: +61 8 6241 2700.

CONTENTS

FOREWORD

There is nothing more obnoxious to the soul than an organization with a monopoly that feeds off the smugness of its own complacency. There is nothing more debilitating than to be part of a church which, having left her first love, has been taken hostage by the tradition of men and fallen short of demonstrating the glory of God.

The glory of God is that He is good. He is personal, intentional and above all else, highly relational. Full of joy and gladness. He has an easy grace. The price has been paid, mercy is overflowing.

Love conquers everything, yet in the church we are not overwhelmed by the majesty of heaven. We are as petty, mean and small-minded as the people we hope to save. Despite incredible access to a higher form of life, godliness and splendor, we use the relational métier of earth rather than the compelling beauty that we discover in the Godhead.

We are an inauthentic generation living in a world where the organ for receptivity of truth has radically changed. In prior times it was the ear. People came to church to hear the Word of God expounded in teaching and preaching. People were open to talking and listening regarding spiritual truths.

In a post-modern world the organ for receptivity of the truth is now the eye. We live in a show-and-tell world. People want to see something. In particular, they need to see two things. Firstly, signs and wonders, miracles, healings, prophecy…the signs of "as in heaven, so on earth."

Secondly, they want to know what God is like. They seek an example: "Show us the Father." The church should be able to say as Christ did, "He who has seen me has seen the Father." Such examples are visual, not merely verbal.

John McElroy is a man with a passion to see heaven on earth, full-on biblical Christianity in this day and age. He skillfully takes us through numerous relational scenarios, each of which must be radically practiced if we are to see the Presence of God in our midst.

We cannot ignore the call to be like Jesus. We cannot disregard the command to "love one another as I have loved you" and expect to have a radical experience of heaven.

The church must return to the biblical roots of relationships. This book is an important part of the dialogue that hopefully will return the church to the fulfilling of the first two commandments.

—Graham Cooke

ACKNOWLEDGMENTS

Next to public speaking, writing a book is probably the second most challenging activity for the average human being. I am very grateful to my family, friends and colleagues around the world whose prayers and encouragement have enabled me to complete the task.

First, I am deeply grateful to my wife, Alaine, and son and daughter Toby and Holly for their support and understanding through the many hours of writing, editing, and fine tuning. My love for my children, biological and spiritual, has compelled me to write this book.

My family in the USA deserves special mention because of their sacrifice in releasing me to the great land "down under." My parents, Bill and Lucille, have written the meaning of honor on my heart. My sister Joni and brother Chris have taught me so much about life and what it means to be a big brother.

I am indebted to my colleagues at Churchlands in Perth for their prayers and support by releasing me to write. They are my adopted family. In particular I wish to thank Ron Ings, Fred Boshart, Alwyn Richards and the staff and board. Your constant support and encouragement will never be forgotten.

I particularly want to thank Melissa and Craig Wright; Melissa for her amazing work in editing the final manuscript and Craig for his practical wisdom. Heather Broadway, Penny Hutton, Lila

Nelson and Toby McElroy all made a significant contribution in proofreading the manuscript. Your eyes for detail are awesome! Thanks also to Patrick Sullivan for your counsel and Dave Hack for designing the cover.

Finally, I am so grateful to the wise and godly men and women who have stood with me over the past thirty years. The Lord has given me favor and friendships beyond what I could ever deserve. Doors have opened, wisdom has been modeled and spoken, and I have had the privilege of knowing some of God's most humble and anointed servants in this generation.

Thank you, one and all, for the awesome part you and God have played in shaping my baton.

INTRODUCTION

For too long the church has produced an army of spectators! Every time I hear statistics indicating that 20 percent of Christians do 80 percent of the Lord's work, it leaves me cold. It has been said that churches are filled with willing people—those who are willing to work, and those who are willing to let them. To be suffocated in lethargy was never what Christ intended for His church.

For thirty years, I have been both frustrated by and a victim of a pastor-dependent culture. The saying, "Darned if you do, and darned if you don't," is an apt description of many pastors. I have been criticized for doing too much and for doing too little; for being too controlling or not strict enough, or just plain failing to care for people. No one can be all things to all people. Pastors cannot play all the positions on a team and the Lord never intended it to be this way.

The time has come to pull the plug on autocrats and let the entire team play. Just as the human body becomes flabby and unfit without exercise, the body of Christ needs some toning up. We need to get our seasoned players off the bench and into the game. To that end we are seeing the five-fold ministries of Ephesians 4:11 emerge as teams. With the help of the Holy Spirit, spectators are being transformed into players.

So why now?

In recent decades, we have witnessed a steady erosion of ethics, values and relationships in every strata of society. The church can no longer afford to sit idly by while our youth are seduced by false religion, paganism and lawlessness.

But how can the church influence a world seemingly hell bent on rejecting its message? The answer is straightforward: it can only happen through the transforming power and presence of Jesus in ordinary people like you and me.

We all have to return to the single factor that built the early church. Relationship is what the church can and should do best. There is no group or religion in the world that can even begin to compare with the church's potential to empower people through relationships, because of Christ in us!

At present, God's people are losing the battle for the hearts and minds of the upcoming generation. The enemy wants to stop the baton of faith being passed from one generation to the next. He wants to intimidate the older folk and distract the younger. He uses tools of suspicion and indifference to drive a wedge between them. The result is a perceived generation gap. His plan is to stop spiritual succession.

A unified church is the greatest threat to the enemy's divide-and-conquer campaign. In every Christian congregation sits a vast, untapped army of spiritual fathers and mothers. The church's greatest challenge is to mobilize these millions to turn their hearts toward the generations coming after them. This can only happen through one-on-one, loving, empowering intergenerational rela-tionships.

All around us young people are waiting and hoping for some-one to take an interest in them. We can abdicate this responsibility to the world and the enemy, or take advantage of this season of grace to see the generations unite and the tide of lawlessness swept back in our land. The soil is right for planting into the hearts of the young. We are about to discover the power of spiritual suc-cession.

PART ONE

A New Season of Grace

See, I will send you the prophet Elijah before that great and dreadful day of the Lord comes. He will turn the hearts of the fathers to their children, and the hearts of the children to their fathers; or else I will come and strike the land with a curse.

—Malachi 4:5–6

THINGS HAVE GOT TO CHANGE!

One generation will commend your works to another; they will tell of your mighty acts.   —Psalm 145:4

The important thing in life is not so much where we stand, as in what direction we are moving.

—Oliver Wendell Holmes

We are entering one of the greatest seasons of God's grace in two thousand years. This season will see the church reformed and transformed. God is releasing His grace to fulfil the prophecy of Malachi 4:5–6. We are about to see a knitting together of the hearts of the older and younger generations. For this to happen, some things have got to change!

When I was nineteen years old, I had a vision from God that changed my life. A Christian friend and I were praying alone one night at a coffee house. It was a difficult time in my life, and I was desperately seeking God's guidance. After about an hour of fervent prayer, I had a vision of Jesus Christ standing in front of me.

When I looked into his face, all I could see was a blinding white light. Despite the brightness, I sensed an incredible warmth and acceptance from the Lord. Jesus then held out a golden shepherd's crook and spoke an inaudible word into my spirit, "This is what you will be in my hands." He invited me to take hold of the crook. I did.

Since that day, I have never had any doubt as to the direction I should go in life. God revealed His Word to me with such indisputable clarity that I was certain of His call to the ministry. Within days following the vision, I shifted from pre-law studies to a course that would help me enter theological seminary.

THE BATON WAS NOT MINE TO KEEP. The fact that Jesus handed me a shepherd's crook was highly significant. For me, the crook was like a baton that I would carry most of my life. Eventually, the Lord would reveal that the baton was not mine to keep. Someday my task would be to pass this golden crook to men and women in future generations.

The task of every Christian is to pass on the baton of God's Word to the next generation. This book has been written with two kinds of people in mind. Those who wish to become spiritual fathers and mothers, and those who are seeking to find them. Not since the days of the early church has God's grace been so favorable for this to happen. We are about to discover why.

THE LAST WORDS OF MALACHI

When reading the Bible, I was always perplexed by the abrupt ending of the book of the prophet Malachi. Why did the Holy Spirit finish the Old Testament with such a stark and cryptic prophecy? Malachi 4:5–6 speaks of a future reality when the hearts of the fathers turn to the children and children to the fathers.

I sought the Lord about this. I believe He showed me Malachi 4 would be fulfilled in two ways. The first time was through the ministry of John the Baptist and the early church. The second fulfillment would come by an apostolic move within the church prior to Christ's second coming.

Regarding the first fulfillment, in Luke 1:17 an angel appeared to Zechariah, John the Baptist's father, and prophesied regarding John's ministry, that "he will go on before the Lord in the spirit and power of Elijah, to turn the hearts of the fathers to the children and the disobedient to the wisdom of the righteous—to make ready a people prepared for the Lord." John the Baptist did indeed come in the spirit and power of Elijah. His tenacious challenging of hearts and message of repentance prepared the way for the Messiah.

Like the prophet Elijah, John challenged the people of Israel to turn back to God. He confronted the ruling religious leaders, reminding them that they were only caretakers of the Law until the promised Messiah came. Many of these religious leaders prided themselves on their position and influence. They lorded it over the people. John exposed their pride and called them to repent and humble themselves before God.

John's message was foundational to Jesus' gospel proclamation of the coming kingdom of God. The gospel, empowered and demonstrated by the Holy Spirit, shaped the church we read of in Acts 2. A ragtag bunch of people became a family community who lived life with each other and experienced a unity of heart between all the generations. Consequently, the early church was highly relational and, as we see with Paul and Timothy, one generation passed the baton successfully to the next.

Eventually the church became distracted and lost its relational focus. By the fourth century, Christianity had been embraced as the state religion of the Roman Empire. The church became political and evolved into an institution having great influence and wealth.

Those at the top, the professional clergy, were uninterested in passing their privileges to the rank and file. They eventually saw the world as divided into two arenas: sacred and secular. Because the two rarely mixed, institutionalism increased and relationships decreased. Church bureaucracy was born!

As the church and clergy became more exclusive, God sent reformers to turn the church back to its first love. By the sixteenth century, Martin Luther pressed for reform by proclaiming justification by faith and the priesthood of all believers. John Wesley followed by pointing the church toward personal holiness and the need for conversion.

The Pentecostal revivalists of the twentieth century were mocked as holy rollers but eventually succeeded in bringing the ministry and gifts of the Holy Spirit back to the church's radar screen. Each reformer spoke to a deficiency of the church in their day.

A COMEDY OF ERRORS

Today, God is calling our attention to the relational gap between the generations. Fathers and sons, mothers and daughters have not always bonded with each other as God intended. Malachi makes it clear that when the hearts of fathers and children are estranged from one another, a curse strikes the land.[1] While this curse takes many forms in society, it also affects the church. Many congregations today are dying because there are few sons and daughters to carry the baton of church leadership.

It is apparent that large numbers of young people are not interested in what churches are offering. They perceive that Christianity is irrelevant, stuck in the dark ages—caught in a time warp of traditionalism and preoccupied with institutional survival.

This perception is reinforced whenever church leaders make reference to youth as the church of the future. While intended as a compliment, young people often interpret this to mean there is no place for them in the church of today. Because traditional churches are unable to attract youth, they are failing to pass on the baton to those who, in previous generations, kept the flame of Christianity alive and glowing.

The truth is, some churches have connected with youth and are vibrant and growing. However, the vast majority are losing ground. I'm not saying that having a vibrant youth element means you are heading in the right direction! Some churches have reacted against the traditional model. Instead, they have sought to attract young people by being more culturally relevant—having a youth worship band and changing to more contemporary songs. These things are not wrong in and of themselves. They deal with the external but they will never be a replacement for one-on-one, empowering relationships.

I grew up in a denominational church and consider myself fortunate to have been part of a great youth group. The pastors took an active part and built relationships with the kids. We developed a celebration service that was presented in churches all around the nation. The level of sharing, intimacy, and God-focused activity within our group was excellent.

Over the years I have gradually re-established contact with many friends from my teenage years. What has surprised and saddened me is to see that many of them who were once so on fire for God have stopped attending church. At first I just blamed people for being lazy or lukewarm, but then I started to ask some tough questions. I was really upset that my Christian friends were no longer walking with God.

Looking back, I can now see that my home church's youth group was weak in two areas: pastor dependence and multiplication of leaders. When our pastors left the church, the group lost most of its momentum. We had become very pastor dependent and we looked to them constantly for guidance and encouragement. They were the cheerleaders who kept us going for God.

The second weakness was a lack of succession in the leadership team. When our youth leaders got tired or moved away, no one had been raised up to take their place. Every leader had to begin building from scratch. Comparisons were constantly made between our old leaders and those who struggled to take their place. I faced a rude awakening. The youth group that had been so influential in my decision to become a pastor had been built on very shaky foundations.

So what did I do? In my first church, and second church, and current church, I simply repeated the same flawed youth ministry model I had learned in my teens. My transition from youth leader to pastor led me to assume that programs that were successful with youth could now be expanded to include adults. And guess what? They worked at first, but eventually failed.

It's terrible when you have to admit that your leadership is flawed. My first clue was when churches subsided in numbers and enthusiasm when I left to lead another church. The second clue was the number of ministries in our church that fell apart when the leaders either left or burned out. The third clue, the clincher, was that my relationships with others lacked warmth and depth. I had become so task and goal-oriented that people frustrated me when they didn't perform to my standards.

Like many of my contemporaries in ministry, I became caught up in a race to ascend the ladder. Looking back, I had built lots of facades but few real foundations for others. In reality, I had simply perpetuated the thing I desperately wanted to avoid, building a pastor-dependent church that would suffer and decline when I moved on.

So what was my blind spot? It was lacking the wisdom and motivation to spend more time actually building my life and heart into people. I was truly the product of an institutional mindset that had been passed on through the church for hundreds of years. I was perpetuating a model of ministry and the same lack of spiritual fathering that had been modelled to me. For this I blame no one but myself. I had not pursued relationships that would have enabled others to challenge my actions or speak into my life.

GETTING THE RIGHT PERSPECTIVE

When I received the vision of Jesus handing me the shepherd's crook, I didn't see the entire picture. Like many young people, I thought the call of God was about me, my vision, my ministry, and going out to change the world. I failed to see myself on a continuum of God's people in every generation who were followers of Jesus Christ. God's priority is not possession, it's about succession.

Short-term thinking is rife in western society. Most people live only from weekend to weekend and fail to prepare adequately for the future. As a young Christian, I thought the second coming of Christ would happen almost immediately, and wondered if I would even have the chance to get married!

We need to understand our place in the continuum of history. One day God showed me a picture of myself running in a marathon with thousands of other runners. I was only one in a series of runners who had been called to carry the baton of God's revelation since the inception of the church.

Then God took me to a time in the future and He replayed the segment of my life when Jesus handed me the golden shepherd's crook. I was so eager to receive it and so enthralled with possessing it that I didn't hear the second part of what He said that day, "But it's not yours to keep." God is so wonderful; after thirty years He replayed the part of the video that I'd missed in the original vision.

MY CANDLE LOSES NOTHING WHEN IT LIGHTS ANOTHER.

For three decades, I held on tightly to my shepherd's crook and didn't even think of passing it on. Thank God for his mercy to a presumptuous, ambitious, and independent man like me! I now see things differently; instead of organizing programs, I want to build empowering relationships.

Rather than be insecure in the success of others, all I really want is to be a good dad and see others advance God's kingdom beyond what I have been able to achieve. Finally, I have come to realize my candle loses nothing when it lights another. It's a good place to be!

We church leaders need to stop holding on to our shepherd crooks and start giving ourselves away to the younger generations. They are crying out for just a crumb of our time—to hear our stories, to feel our wounds and touch the pulse of our passion for Jesus. We only have a window of time with our sons and daughters to influence their perspectives. Let's grasp this moment of opportunity and impart a lasting legacy of God's Word.

In this new season of grace, God the Father is raising an army of spiritual mothers and fathers who will refuse to take their mantles to the grave. They have caught a vision of the power of spiritual succession and know it holds the key to the future of the church until Jesus returns. The choice is obvious, succession or extinction.

CHAPTER ONE—REALITY CHECK

- If you're a church leader, ask yourself this question. Are God's people dependent on you to an unhealthy degree? What would happen if you left?

- Many people view Malachi 4 as having been fulfilled only during the time of John the Baptist. Can you see the importance of its fulfillment in our present day?

- Take a reality check of the relationships in your local fellowship. Do the generations relate to each other or are they all in separate camps?

CHAPTER TWO

LEAVING A LEGACY

A good man leaves an inheritance for his children's children.

—Proverbs 13:22

A hundred times every day I remind myself that my inner and outer life depend on the labors of other men, living and dead, and that I must exert myself in order to give in the same measure as I have received and am still receiving.

—Albert Einstein

What we leave behind as a legacy reveals our priorities. It shouts how we want to be remembered. It unveils whether we pointed to Jesus or us. It is the testimony of God's work in our lives; the spiritual inheritance or baton that we leave to others. God's plan for the church has always been that one generation would pass the baton of the testimony of Jesus to the next generation until His return. You and I are just one in a series of runners...

When I was growing up, my father would take me to watch our local high school athletes compete in track and field events. At these track meets, teams competed in events like the high jump, pole vault, shot put, discus throw, and various types of marathon runs, sprints and relays.

When I was old enough to compete, our school track coach selected me to take part in the 100-yard dash and 440-yard relay. Both races required speed and coordination. While the dash was a single person race, the relay was a test of speed and teamwork. After sprinting 110 yards, each runner would pass a lightweight, hollow baton to the next runner.

I still remember the adrenaline surge as the starter shouted, "On your marks, ready, set!" He fired his gun and then off we shot in front of a cheering crowd.

In the 440-yard relay, races were won or lost at the handing of the baton. To drop the baton meant losing the race. All the hard work, all the after-school training, everything could be dashed with a single fumble. Rule Number One of relay events was: NEVER DROP THE BATON!

The same is true of life. Life is not a 100-yard dash; it's a relay where we pass a legacy to those who follow us. We have not successfully finished the race of life until we have passed on our baton to the next generation.

A baton is much more than a lightweight hollow tube. It represents the spiritual inheritance we have in Christ that we have accumulated in our lifetime. Your baton is the sum of all the lessons, insights, wisdom, counsel, character and spiritual anointing that you have gained. The person you've become and the sacrifices you have made combine to form a rich deposit of God's living word in you. Your baton is your spiritual legacy.

THE MEANING OF LEGACY

To understand legacy let's look at Proverbs 13:22.

A good man leaves an inheritance for his children's children.

A legacy is an inheritance for your children and your children's children. It's easier to think of this in terms of the wealth we leave behind when we die. We are all aware of parents who have spent a lifetime carving a position of influence and wealth only to leave it to children who squander it in a very short time. This comes about because the right values have not been passed on to the children and so they've wasted the opportunity.

Far too many inheritances are short-lived. Parents have been better at making money than teaching their children how to steward wealth wisely. As Socrates so aptly put it, "Could I climb to the highest place in Athens, I would lift my voice and proclaim: 'Fellow citizens, why do you turn and scrape every stone to gather wealth, and take so little care of your children   to whom one day you must relinquish it all?' "

Leaving a spiritual legacy is similar. The focus is on the benefits for the generations coming after you rather than for yourself. It requires long-term thinking, not short-term thinking.

ONLY WHAT IS BUILT WITH ETERNITY IN MIND WILL LAST.

Far too often we hear of a great man or woman of God and the incredible ministry they've built, only to see the whole thing fracture at the seams when they die. The Lord warns us in 1 Corinthians 3:10–13 to be careful how we build, as the quality of our work will be tested at the end of the age. Only what is built with eternity in mind will last and receive a reward.

In *The 21 Irrefutable Laws of Leadership*, John Maxwell speaks of four types of accomplishment in a leader's life:

- ACHIEVEMENT comes to someone when he is able to *do great things for himself*;

- SUCCESS comes when he empowers followers to *do great things with him*;

- SIGNIFICANCE comes when he develops leaders to *do great things for him*; but

- a LEGACY is created when a person puts his organization into the position to *do great things without him.*[2]

The aim of legacy is succession. However, many of today's leaders focus on achievement and success. A minority go on to the higher level of significance and building dream teams to accomplish their vision. Few seem concerned with enabling others to do great things without them. I will never forget the lessons I learned about this in my first church.

MY FIRST CHURCH

I became a pastor at the age of twenty. Like most other pastors in my denomination, I trained at a theological seminary for three years. Seminary was where I received *formal* academic training. Most of what I now remember came from an *informal* school; the school of experience in actual ministry situations.

For four years, I drove 140 miles each weekend to serve a small congregation of about 150 people. I learned to be a pastor through hands-on experience.

My duties were diverse: weddings and funerals, leading Bible studies, coordinating a youth group of twenty kids, and preaching sermons each Sunday morning. While I did have other pastors I could turn to, much of what I learned was through trial and error.

When I trained for the ministry, little was said about the need for spiritual fathers and mothers. The focus was on ministerial formation, academic subjects, exams, and how to prepare sermons using proper biblical exegesis. Because our denomination had high standards for ordination, many had a fear of not making the grade. Every pastor just assumed he had to learn to stand on his own.

Looking back, I can now see that my major focus was on *achievement* and *success*. It really didn't enter my mind to think about what would happen to the congregation when I left. I gave little thought to passing on my baton and being a spiritual father. The relationships I had in the church were based on friendship and getting things done.

Everything went pretty smoothly until, after seven years, I received an invitation to pastor a church in Perth, Australia, my wife's home city. Within six months God made it clear that I should accept the position.

Announcing my resignation was difficult. The people had become like family and were very dependent upon our leadership. In hindsight, I failed in a number of ways.

- I had not spent time mentoring and empowering leaders who could take over when I left the church.

- I had not assisted the church in finding a successor to myself.

- I had not addressed destructive patterns of behavior and conflict in the church membership.

- While I had reasonably fulfilled my pastoral responsibilities, I had simply perpetuated a pastor-dependent culture.

Unfortunately, failures like mine are often repeated throughout churches everywhere. I had no thought of leaving a legacy and nobody ever challenged me on the subject.

Many of us don't like the idea of legacy. It reminds us we are mortal; that our life is fleeting. It causes us to reflect on how we have lived and on how we are living. Some of us would like to convince ourselves that legacy is something to act on near the end of our life. We don't like the idea of passing on the baton if it means another will rise higher. We don't want to miss out!

In view of the widespread decline in church attendance, we must think outside the box and start on the path of leaving a legacy. For this to happen, our priorities have to change. Colin Noyes of CoachNet Pacific makes an astute observation: "Life's greatest deception is to think that by doing the same thing, in the same way, over and over, we will ultimately get a different result."[3]

We can no longer assume that spiritual succession will just happen. To shift the rudder of the church will take focus, time and courage. We must return to the model of legacy that Jesus set for us. He raised disciples who could multiply themselves and take His message to the ends of the earth. He passed on His baton effectively, and so must we.

Returning to the model of Jesus will not happen overnight. It will require a change of mindset for the church to become less institutional and more relational. In the next chapter, we examine how this change can begin to take place.

CHAPTER TWO—REALITY CHECK

- What does your baton look like? What are some of the lessons and insights you have learned that would be worth passing on to others?

- Maxwell's *Four Types of Accomplishment* relate to all of us, not just leaders. Which type best describes you at this point in your life?

- Are you leaving a legacy? Is it of eternal value? Consider making a list now of what needs to change.

CHAPTER THREE

THE CHURCH'S DILEMMA

Every day they continued to meet together in the temple courts. They broke bread in their homes and ate together with glad and sincere hearts, praising God and enjoying the favor of all the people. —Acts 2:46–47

Life's greatest deception is to think that by doing the same thing, in the same way, over and over; we will ultimately achieve a different result. —Colin Noyes

Why has much of the church moved from the relational family of Acts 2 into an impersonal institution? Self focus has seeped in, dowsing our first love. What was once vibrant has become embedded in ritual; our passion for winning souls has taken second place to guarding our comfort. Things have got to change! Our heavenly Father is kindly calling us back to basics. And it all begins with relationship...

Growing up in familiar surroundings can often make us blind to flaws in our environment. We can be enamoured by our family, our friends, or our church to such an extent that we are unable to see things objectively and make positive changes when they are required.

In the first chapter, I recounted an experience in my teenage years in our church youth group. I really enjoyed the group and grew spiritually. Only years later did I discover some flaws in our leadership style. Until I discovered the flaws, I simply repeated many of the same mistakes when I eventually became a pastor.

Most of us are creatures of habit. We become accustomed to doing things in a certain way. Once a pattern is established, it becomes difficult to change. This is particularly true in our approach to our faith.

Traditions, rituals, programs and ways of doing things can easily become more enticing and more comfortable than being obedient to God. They can delude us into thinking we are fulfilling God's will. To illustrate this, let's look at one of my favorite contemporary parables taken from life on the Australian beach.

The parable of the surf-lifesaving club

On a dangerous seacoast where shipwrecks often occur, there was once a crude little lifesaving station. The building was just a hut, and there was only one boat, but the few devoted members kept a constant watch over the sea. With no thought for their own safety, they went out day and night, tirelessly searching for the lost. Some of those who were saved, and various others in the surrounding area, wanted to become associated with the station and give their time, money and effort for the support of its work. New boats were bought and new crews trained. The little lifesaving station grew.

Some of the members of the lifesaving station were unhappy that the building was so crude and poorly equipped. They felt that a more comfortable place should be provided as the first refuge of those saved from the sea. They replaced the emergency cots with beds and put better furniture in the enlarged building. Now the lifesaving station became a popular gathering place for its members and they decorated it beautifully and furnished it exquisitely, because they used it as a sort of club.

Fewer members were now interested in going to sea on lifesaving missions, so they hired lifeboat crews to do this work. The lifesaving motif still prevailed in the club's decorations, and there was a liturgical lifeboat in the room where the club initiations were held.

About this time a large ship was wrecked off the coast, and the hired crews brought in boatloads of cold, wet and half-drowned people. They were dirty and sick and some of them had different colored skin. The beautiful new club was in chaos. So the property committee immediately had a shower house built outside the club where victims of shipwreck could be cleaned up before coming inside.

At the next meeting, there was a split in the club membership. Most of the members wanted to stop the club's lifesaving activities as they were unpleasant and a hindrance to the normal social life of the club. Some members insisted that lifesaving was their primary purpose and pointed out that they were still called a lifesaving station. But they were voted down and told that if they wanted to save the lives of the various kinds of people who were shipwrecked in those waters, they could begin their own lifesaving station down the coast. And so they did.

SHIPWRECKS ARE FREQUENT IN THOSE WATERS, BUT MOST OF THE PEOPLE DROWN!

As the years went by, the new station experienced the same changes that had occurred in the old. It evolved into a club, and yet another lifesaving station was founded. History continued to repeat itself, and if you visit that sea coast today, you will find a number of exclusive clubs along that shore. Shipwrecks are frequent in those waters, but most of the people drown![4]

The parable of the surf-lifesaving club bears a strong resemblance to the history of many churches. Over the years the focus of the Western church has shifted away from relationship and winning souls and more towards social programs and institutional concerns. Instead of being God's house, many congregations resemble a supermarket. Believers are presented with a smorgasbord of things to be involved in. Self-sacrifice, being a servant and taking up the cross of Christ appear to have become optional extras.

Too often the church is inundated with programs and mundane activities that produce little fruit and experience only a small measure of God's power. We need to re-evaluate this constant busyness. It is easy to lose sight of the purpose for which the church was originally established. Consider this segment from Acts 2:42–47.

> They devoted themselves to the apostles' teaching and to the fellowship, to the breaking of bread and to prayer. Everyone was filled with awe, and many wonders and miraculous signs were done by the apostles. All the believers were together and had everything in common. Selling their possessions and goods, they gave to anyone as he had need. Every day they continued to meet together in the temple courts. They broke bread in their homes and ate together with glad and sincere hearts, praising God and enjoying the favor of all the people. And the Lord added to their number daily those who were being saved.

How church life has changed since Bible days! It's hard to imagine a prolonged time in the church when wonders and miraculous signs were commonplace. Believers had everything in common and were willing to sell what they had to help others with needs. What about a daily increase of those being saved? Reports of life in the early church are almost beyond comprehension! Why have things changed? How is it that we have become so ineffective?

THE CURRENT DILEMMA

The problem with people in the parable of the surf-lifesaving club was selfishness and self-centered behavior. This caused them to lose perspective and become ineffective in their primary work of saving lives. Instead of putting the interests of victims of shipwreck first, they began to put their own comfort and agenda first.

The reason we can relate to this parable is because we see it so often in the world and in the church. The driving force of Western society is the pursuit of self, ambition, and pleasure. We live in a culture obsessed with self!

Whether we know it or not, many Christians have become like the frog in the kettle. If you want to kill a frog, put it in a kettle of cold water and gradually turn up the heat over a long period of time. As the temperature of the water in the kettle slowly increases, the frog becomes sluggish and, over time, happily boils to death without a struggle. On the other hand, if you try putting a frog in a pot of hot water, it will quickly leap frog out of there!

The church's declining influence can be traced to its inability to understand what is happening in society and to present knowing Christ as the only solution. The world around us has changed drastically in the past few decades. Our society has been bombarded with at least four unbiblical worldviews that need to be exposed, not embraced by the church. These four worldly philosophies are: relativism, hedonism, individualism, and consumerism.

Relativism teaches that all truth is relative; there are no absolute truths or values. Truth is flexible and determined by what seems right to an individual at the time.

Hedonism advocates that happiness is found through the seeking and enjoyment of pleasure. It is summed up by the phrase, "If it feels good, do it!"

Individualism states that self-interest and self-expression are the highest goals of humanity. The emphasis is on the individual rather than the community.

Finally, **consumerism** believes that most important human needs can be met through the buying and selling of goods and services. Advertisements promise happiness and fulfillment whenever we worship at the temples of consumerism: shopping malls!

Collectively, these four unbiblical philosophies exert an insidious influence on the thinking and behavior of the average person in Western society. This false wisdom makes Christianity and church involvement less attractive to the majority of people who have embraced the spirit of this age. The Christian teachings of the cross, denying self, honoring others above yourself, and obeying Jesus' commands are unpalatable to the carnal mind.

The antidote to relativism, hedonism, individualism and consumerism is the Word of God. The enemy wants us to substitute his lies for God's Word. Like the frog in the kettle, Christians can gradually embrace unbiblical values as acceptable if they do not know God's ways and thoughts. This leads to compromise with the world and renders us ineffective in our witness of Christ. It is imperative that we return to the foundation of God's Word to test the barrage of lies that our society dishes up as truth and wisdom.

THREE DECEPTIONS

Over the years I have noticed three recurring deceptions that threaten to take Christians off the front line and render them ineffective: self-satisfaction, passivity and distractions. In the parable of the sower,[5] Jesus compared the kingdom of heaven to a farmer who went out to sow seed. The seed fell in four places.

- Along the path where birds came and ate it up. This represents the person who hears the message about the kingdom but doesn't understand it so the enemy comes and snatches away what was sown in the heart.

- On rocky places where the soil was shallow. This speaks of the person who hears the message and receives it with joy but, because his faith has no roots, it lasts only a short time.

- Among the thorns that grew up and choked the plants. This speaks of the worries of life and the deceitfulness of wealth that choke faith.

- In good soil that produced a large crop. This speaks of the person who hears the Word, understands it and builds faith into others.

Self-satisfaction is a form of pride that makes us resistant to change. Pride is the enemy's greatest deception. It inhibits God's grace. We read in 1 Peter 5:5 that "God opposes the proud but gives grace to the humble." Self-satisfied people don't need any-thing or anyone. Like the path in the first part of the parable, their hearts are often hardened and unreceptive to hearing the truth. They usually have all the answers and are not teachable.

Whenever God wants to change something, He increases His grace accordingly. But, if we are satisfied with the status quo, we can easily miss or resist God's grace when change is required. Like the people in the surf-lifesaving club parable, self-satisfaction will cause us to move out of love and out of God's will, and leave us with a hollow lifeless reminder of what we once had.

The second deception is passivity. People who are passive be-lieve life owes them something. Again the emphasis is on self. Like the seed that fell in shallow rocky soil, their faith does not have depth as it is not rooted in the love of God. When difficult times come, it is easier to abandon the truth and go with the flow.

Passivity lulls us toward laziness. It whispers, "Someone else will do it." It advocates not rocking the boat. It seeks comfort above sacrifice but its reward is futility. Shallowness is evident when we expect God to make all the moves. God wants us to draw near to Him, and THEN He will draw near to us.[6] Allowing passivity in our lives is an open invitation to the enemy to steal away the promises of our purpose!

HOLD TO THE IMPORTANT RATHER THAN THE URGENT.

Distractions are like the thorns that grow up and choke our faith. Unless we maintain focus on the things of God, we can become distracted by small issues that are not important. Some of life's greatest distractions are busyness, worry, ungodly relationships, unrealistic expectations, and chasing after money. Each of these can effectively keep us pouring out our energy and life purpose. The danger is in the trade-off. In taking up one thing, another is neglected. We do well if we hold to the important rather than the urgent.

If our view of God is obscured through pride, distractions and passivity, the church will reflect an institutional mindset and attitude. If on the other hand, our passion is for Jesus and becoming like Him, we will seek to pour our lives into others, in selfless love. Only in this way, as hearts are changed, will the church become more relational and less like a sanctified club.

GETTING BACK TO THE IMPORTANT

Nineteen years ago I was led to pastor a group of forty men and women who planted a church in Perth, Western Australia. I can still remember the first four or five years, so filled with enthusiasm and believing our church could really make a difference. I still believe that! Our journey began with a single step, but it was a huge step into the unknown.

Enthusiasm often proves contagious. The little fellowship began to grow. One person at a time, then family by family, I watched our little church double in size every year for the first five years. What started as a group of about forty adults grew to well over 500 within five years.

The path to 500 was quite an adventure. As we approached the one-hundred mark, we needed a children's ministry facility. So we rented another building and hired a young man to oversee it. Soon we needed to enlarge our small group ministry so we hired a part-time coordinator. Then I needed a secretary. Then we needed counsellors. Then we needed more programs and more volunteers to run them. Then, then, then!

One of the greatest pitfalls of church life and growth is what I call the tyranny of the urgent. This happens when the urgent or pressing issues of life start to overshadow important things. As our church grew, I felt a lot of pressure to keep on top of the needs of a growing church.

I love leadership and organizing activities. For many years, I found an outlet for my gift by living on a treadmill of meetings and administrative activities. Unfortunately, I left little time for building quality relationships.

MANY CHRISTIANS WOULD RATHER *ESCAPE* THAN *ENGAGE* OTHERS.

I have since discovered that the most effective style of leadership is to raise and release others to do the work of ministry. The time I spend building into emerging leaders and helping them fine tune is far more productive than when I used to do things by myself. I can't begin to tell you how much more I enjoy ministry since deciding to shift priorities away from attending meetings and more toward building into people.

Sadly, for many Christians, life has become so busy that they would rather *escape* than *engage* others. Busyness kills relationship and is the perfect breeding ground for distractions, tiredness and futility. Some of us would rather be always doing and never resting, and so play straight into the enemy's hands.

The enemy's major weapon against the church and the world has always been deception. Deception involves getting people to believe a lie and then act it out as if it were true. God, the author of truth, wants His people to be freed from the falsehoods of unbiblical thinking and to avoid the pitfalls of self-satisfaction, passivity and distractions.

But only when God's people embrace the cross of Christ, die to self, and pour out their lives in selfless love, will we begin to see the tide turn and the church restored to the vibrancy we see in Acts 2.

CHAPTER THREE—REALITY CHECK

- Have you ever been part of a group like the one in the parable of the surf-lifesaving club? What did you learn?

- Consider church life as recorded in Acts 2. What would you like to see more of in the church today?

- Have you ever struggled with self-satisfaction, passivity or distractions? What are you doing to address this?

CHAPTER FOUR

Bridging the Gap

And let us consider how we may spur one another on toward love and good deeds. Let us not give up meeting together, as some are in the habit of doing, but let us encourage one another —and all the more as you see the Day approaching.　　　　　　　—Hebrews 10:24–25

No one is useless in this world who lightens the burden of it to anyone else.　　　　　　　—Charles Dickens

In any relationship, someone has to take the initiative. The Bible tells us that we love because God first loved us. He intended that first the hearts of the older generations would turn toward the younger. God's love, expressed through us, bridges the relational gap between the generations. In this season, a multitude of spiritual fathers and mothers must learn to love their spiritual sons and daughters and pass on the testimony of Christ.

Our God is highly relational. He wants to have relationship with us, and wants us to relate lovingly to one another. We are family. As we love God, love each other and make disciples of the nations, we satisfy the Father's heart. God's plan is that His children enjoy the same unity and harmony that exists in the Trinity.

The Bible chronicles the progression of God's plan. The Old Testament begins by recounting God's relationship with the patriarchs, judges, prophets and kings. He is known as the God of Abraham, Isaac and Jacob; the God of the generations.

The focus then shifts to relationship with a nation of people, Israel, who had been prepared to receive the Messiah, Jesus Christ, whom God would send to them. From there, the message of God's desire for His people to be restored in relationship with Him would be taken throughout the world by the church. The church is to be a reflection of God's love relationship with His people, through His Son Jesus.

As a bridge between the Old and New Testaments, Malachi 4 highlights a *grace* that can only be fulfilled under the New Covenant. As Jesus turned His heart toward God's children, the hearts of the children were returned to their heavenly Father. He embodied the Father's heart by laying down His life for us. The first disciples followed His example, and love for one another became the basis of early church life.

Jesus' ministry reveals an important sequence in forming intergenerational relationships. First, the hearts of the fathers must be turned to the children. Fathers and mothers will usually need to take the initiative in establishing relationship with their protégés.

As relationships are established, the children's hearts will soften and they will grow to value and pursue relationship with their fathers and mothers. Then a shift must occur. We must teach our sons and daughters to take *initiative* in maintaining relationship. The reason for this is that they will someday need to take initiative toward their sons and daughters. If we deprive them of this experience, they will expect others to come to them first.

Intergenerational relationships create the momentum for passing on the baton. There are three things we need to understand about these relationships.

- They take place best through spiritual parents.

- They provide an antidote to discouragement.

- They enable us to receive a spiritual inheritance that would otherwise be unavailable to us.

WHY WE NEED SPIRITUAL PARENTS

God's plan has always been that one generation would pass His Word to the next. This is why we need spiritual fathers and mothers. They enable us to reap in fields where we have not sown, and help us to avoid many pitfalls on the road of life.

Spiritual parents help keep us on the road to maturity in Christ. Many times people stray from God because the enemy attacks their self-confidence. In times of warfare, we need allies who can stand with us and help bolster our defences. In Ecclesiastes 4:12 we read, "Though one may be overpowered, two can defend themselves. A cord of three strands is not quickly broken." Spiritual parents join with us to make a formidable alliance. They encourage us, stand with God in defending us, and provide valuable perspective into the issues we face.

I have discovered three recurring reasons why people plateau in their spiritual growth.

- They do not have a true perspective of God's character.

- They lack mentors, parents, spouses, teachers, and friends who could give them the consistent encouragement they needed during times of trial.

- They failed to recognize their accomplishments and victories, or had an amplified view of their failures.

God wants to put people in our lives who can administer His antidotes to discouragement. Spiritual parents do this in three ways: by keeping us connected to God, giving us honest feedback, and helping us remember the positives.

Three antidotes to discouragement

Spiritual parents help us connect with God. They are there to encourage and push us, if necessary, to draw closer to God. Sometimes our biggest mistake is waiting for God to come our way! James 4:8 says, "Come near to God and He will come near to you." If we will take the initiative, THEN He will reveal Himself to us. Spiritual mothers and fathers hold us accountable to press into God.

When we come close to God we get a clearer perspective on our situation. The enemy is the father of lies. His tactic is to lie to us about our situation, get us to focus on ourselves and then get us to act out the lie. He loves to separate us from others so he can pick us off!

God always tells us the truth. And what is the truth? The truth is we are valuable and precious. We are unique and have a call on our life. We have a great inheritance that lies ahead. We are not an accident but part of God's great plan. Spiritual parents keep us on the road to improvement by helping us stay connected to God.

Spiritual parents give us honest feedback. We need people who can speak the truth in love. It is one thing to speak the truth; it is another thing to do it in love. Truth should always be sprinkled with grace. Honest feedback needs to be given in a way that builds us up, that corrects and yet affirms us at the same time.

We need fathers and mothers who will be mirrors, to encourage our strengths and correct our weaknesses, and who have a heart to see us improve. Sadly, many people have no one who speaks into their lives. There are at least three reasons for this. It has *not occurred to them to ask* someone to do it; they are looking to the *wrong people* to do it, or they have *made others fear the consequences* of being honest with them.

Most people receive constructive criticism better from people they know and trust. It is in relationship that our insecurities, hurts, fears and hidden agendas are exposed. Honest feedback is better given and received when we are in relationship with others.

Spiritual parents help us remember the positives. Human nature is a funny thing. In the course of a day we can receive ten compliments and one criticism, but which one do we remember? The one criticism! It is so easy for the negative to eclipse the positive in life. We need people who can remind us of what God has done for us in the past and His redemptive purposes for our future.

There are two ways of viewing parents. We can view them as an asset or as a liability. True sons and daughters view parents as an asset. They see parents as their source of inheritance and honor them accordingly. The Lord intends that the inheritance of the godly be passed from generation to generation.[7]

TRUE SONS AND DAUGHTERS VIEW PARENTS AS AN ASSET.

The aim of spiritual succession is to raise godly men and women who can pass their baton to upcoming generations. This ensures a continuity of effective leaders in the church until the Lord returns. But there is much more to consider. Handing over our baton is a supreme act of love, trust, faith, and kindness.

The world, and the upcoming generation, needs to see more of this kind of self-effacing love. The younger generations want to follow the real thing! They desperately want to know that there are faith heroes alive today who will unswervingly hold to Christ, sacrifice all and love all! As John Maxwell once said, "A leader who gathers followers needs to be needed. A leader who raises leaders wants to be succeeded."[8] Only secure leaders empower others and want to leave a legacy.

THE PURPOSE OF A MANTLE

In the Old Testament, a spiritual inheritance was represented by a *mantle*. Although a mantle was simply a cloak, it was symbolic of the ministry anointing that rested on a servant of God.

The Bible speaks of many godly men and women who, at the conclusion of their ministry, passed on their mantle to a successor.

Elijah's mantle was passed to Elisha. Moses passed his to Joshua. Jesus passed His to the apostles. Paul passed his to many others, but most notably to Timothy, his spiritual son.

God's purpose for a mantle is two-fold. First, it gives us the ability to minister His grace during our lifetime. Second, our mantle is meant to be part of the spiritual inheritance that God passes through us to successive generations. Often we have embraced the former but neglected the latter. We have not finished the race of life until we have passed our mantle to others.

Some of life's greatest treasures... must be received as gifts.

Many of life's most profound and memorable lessons are learned, not in a classroom, but through relationships. Some of life's greatest treasures cannot be bought or possessed, but must be received as gifts. I am so grateful for the spiritual deposit that others have placed in my life.

Over the past thirty years, I have developed close friendships with a number of men and women who allowed me to travel with or observe them in ministry. The late John Wimber became like a spiritual father to me and opened my eyes to incredible manifestations of signs and wonders. My friend Francis Frangipane has allowed me to travel with him and witness the grace on his life to establish unity within the body of Christ. His books have fed my passion to become more like Jesus.

I could mention other well known servants of God who have shared their mantles with me. Rick Joyner's and Graham Cooke's prophetic writings have challenged me by profound revelations of God's purposes for the church. Jack Deere and John Chacha are gifted teachers who have unlocked the mysteries of God's Word and fed a passion, making it come alive to me. More recently, John Alley and Rita Johnson have modelled the heart of an apostle. God designed us to learn from the experiences of others.

Every Christian has a mantle and God expects us to pass it on to others. You don't have to be famous to have a mantle. We should never think that because we are not well known, or a leader, that we have nothing to pass on. God has given each believer a deposit of the Spirit that will bless others. This can only be done through relationship.

IMPARTATION

I recently read *The Heavenly Man*,[9] the incredible story of Chinese Christian Brother Yun. The book reads like a contemporary re-enactment of the book of Acts! Coincidentally, shortly after I finished reading his book, our church was contacted and asked if Brother Yun could speak one evening in our auditorium. Of course, we jumped at the opportunity.

The 1,500 seat auditorium was packed. People flocked from far and near to hear of the wonderful move of God in China. Over 1,000 watched him on video screens because we could not fit them inside!

At the end of the meeting, Brother Yun invited my wife and me to the platform. He then prayed fervently that God's blessing would be imparted to us.

It was like a lightning bolt went through my stomach! Something of the Spirit was imparted that night and I have never been the same since. My fervor for mission has increased, as has my sense of boldness and conviction. These are the same qualities I observed in Brother Yun.

The dictionary defines *impart* as "to grant a share of; bestow; to make known, disclose; to pass on, transmit." If we honor those God has placed in authority, we receive a portion of their mantle or anointing. When we received God's servant, we also received an immediate impartation of the Spirit.

Impartation can also happen over time. Whenever you place yourself under the spiritual authority of a person or group, it begins a process of gradual impartation. Jesus alluded to this principle in Matthew 10:41:

> Anyone who receives a prophet because he is a prophet will receive a prophet's reward, and anyone who receives a righteous man because he is a righteous man will receive a righteous man's reward.

In this verse, prophets can represent itinerant ministries. While they are often with us for only a short time, prophets can pass God's grace on to us in an instant.

On the other hand, the reward of a righteous man speaks more of those blessings that are passed on to us gradually, often through on-going relationship with spiritual parents. Paul told the Thessalonians that he and his team were, "well pleased to impart...not only the gospel of God but also **our own lives**."[10]

The Lord has an inheritance stored up for us in heaven. The good news is that we can begin tapping into this inheritance while we live on earth. We tap in by receiving the *rewards* or mantles of prophets and righteous men and women. This is for our strengthening to be effective witnesses for Jesus.

WE CANNOT PASS THE BATON OUTSIDE OF RELATIONSHIP.

Many of us have grown up in the information culture of classrooms and lectures. We can easily confuse spiritual maturity with what we know, rather than what we put into practice. Impartation is more than teaching facts and giving information. It often takes time and a high degree of transparency.

Spiritual parenting also requires more than teaching. Much of what we need to pass on is more caught than taught. Think of it. You catch a cold when you're exposed to a virus. Exposure is what causes us to catch what other people have. Ongoing relationships with spiritual fathers and mothers enable us to catch what they've got.

RELATIONSHIPS REQUIRE TIME AND SENSITIVITY

Life changing relationships cannot be superficial; they require time and sharing our deepest thoughts with another human being. This may require a change of lifestyle or daily schedule. For me, this meant spending time sharing with spiritual sons and daughters over breakfast at a time when I am more alert.

The more time we spend in another person's company, the more we begin to emulate their qualities. In a very real sense, we become the company we keep. Remember, our goal in building into sons and daughters is more than growth in knowledge. We also want to impart our passion, character, and the unique deposit of God's Word that we carry within.

Relationships enable us to pass on to others what God has given us. It can take years to build the degree of intimacy needed to share your deepest secrets and lessons of life. People need to see how we respond to life situations. Time in relationship allows others to observe our consistency, integrity, and how we operate under pressure.

Sensitivity enhances relationships, insensitivity will kill them. We must learn to be good listeners and let others have our undivided attention. Good eye contact is essential. Nothing is worse than trying to carry on a conversation with a person who is preoccupied or distracted.

It is also important to respect the dignity of another person. To me this means three things: never belittling a person; keeping confidential information to yourself unless you have been granted permission to do otherwise, and not allowing their reputation to be slandered in your presence.

Many people these days are far too flippant about friendship; they assume it will always be there when they want it. This is not true. I grew up with the belief that you must be a friend to have a friend. Ask yourself, "How can I be a friend to this person? What can I do or say that will build them up and enable them to draw nearer to God?"

Sometimes people need to see that even though we are busy, we want to make quality time for them and their concerns. A portion of my time is spent leading an international network of churches. While I love to meet with leaders face-to-face, this isn't always possible. Most contact with our network ministries must be done by phone or email. Others feel valued when I respond promptly to their emails and calls.

Of course, you cannot use electronic communication as a substitute for real relationship. People are not machines. Regular times of discussion, listening, laughing, eating and praying together form strong bonds. We cannot pass the baton outside of relationship.

Each of us has a choice. We can take the path of self-sufficiency; trying to do and learn everything on our own. Or, we can take God's path of spiritual succession and link with fathers and mothers who impart their wisdom, perspective, experience and encouragement to us.

In the next part of the book we look at making the shift to a church culture that is more relational and less impersonal. It is time the world recognizes we are God's people because of our love for one another, and not because of our criticisms and divisions. It starts with honoring each other.

CHAPTER FOUR—REALITY CHECK

- Have you ever given another person permission to speak into your life? How have you received their feedback?

- Have you viewed your parents as assets or liabilities? Have you ever sensed a relationship gap? If so, was it ever resolved? What could you do now to resolve it?

- How well do you maintain relationship with those who are important in your life? How could you improve?

PART TWO

PASSING ON THE BATON

Even though you have ten thousand guardians in Christ, you do not have many fathers, for in Christ Jesus I became your father through the gospel. Therefore I urge you to imitate me.

—1 Corinthians 4:15–16

BUILDING A CULTURE OF HONOR

Be devoted to one another in brotherly love. Honor one another above yourselves. —Romans 12:10

If I have seen further than other men, it is because I have stood on the shoulders of giants. —Sir Isaac Newton

Whenever a nation is plagued with vandalism and violence, it points to a lack of honor and respect. Dishonor lies at the root of lawlessness. It feeds on selfishness. God wants the culture of the church to be shaped by selfless love. We are called to be His light in the darkness. As we embrace the attitude of Jesus in our lives, honor will be reflected in our relationships. The world will recognize we are His because of our love for one another.

There is often a huge generation gap in society and in the church. Older people feel very uneasy about getting involved in the lives of younger people. They feel intimidated, like they have little to offer. This is understandable, given the huge advances in technology, travel and communication that have taken place over the past half-century. Many older folk feel like they grew up in a bygone era and wonder how to bridge the relational gap when they appear to have so little in common with today's youth.

Younger people, on the other hand, tend to keep their distance from the older generation. Why? Because they sense they have little in common. Their "now" culture of iPods, digital clips, and instant communication is seen as beyond the comprehension or interest of their elders. I have often heard young people say, "After all, what do you talk about to an older person?"

THERE IS ONE GREAT COMMON DENOMINATOR THAT NEVER CHANGES: LOVE.

However, there is one great common denominator that never changes: love. Most people eventually respond when somebody shows that they care for them. God has wired each of us with a deep need for acceptance, belonging and encouragement. Much of the disrespect and mistrust between generations can be traced to a lack of ongoing, caring interaction. We have often taken the selfish and easy path of keeping to ourselves and relating largely to people in our own generation.

In Malachi 4, God speaks of the "hearts of the fathers being **turned** to the children." Quite simply, turning our hearts toward anyone means learning to love them and doing whatever it takes to establish an ongoing intimate relationship. When fathers and mothers turn their hearts toward the children, sooner or later the children THEN respond. In any relationship, someone has to take the initiative.

Within the church, I have often seen older leaders undermine or demean their younger counterparts. It's an attitude that says, "I had to go through tough times, why should they have it any easier?" While testing is important for us all, many older leaders have failed to honor the younger, seeing them as competitors rather than as part of the same team. A lack of honor then fuels resentment.

Spiritual fathers and mothers need to respect and affirm, not criticize the differences between the generations.

The Lord wants His people to reflect honor as the rule, not the exception. Jesus Christ honored others above Himself. He honored His heavenly Father by humbly submitting to His will. He honored His disciples by washing their feet. He honored others by His sacrifice, as the good shepherd who laid down His life for the sheep. When we honor others, we follow in the footsteps of Jesus.

BUT WHAT IS HONOR?

We honor others whenever we show respect or behave in a way that adds value to their life. Honor arises from *gratitude* in our hearts. It can never be forced but can only be given willingly. Gratitude feeds the desire to honor others above ourselves. Honor comes from the realization that another person has enabled you to achieve something you couldn't have done without them. It is this realization that makes us grateful and releases love and humility in our hearts.

Honor stems from an awareness of what God and others have done in our lives. Honor must be taught, explained, and continually re-emphasized to our children. Some parents never speak about honor; they assume their kids will just understand its importance. This is not wise. For most of us, the natural inclination will be to take credit for most of our accomplishments. Children need to be taught generosity, humility, and to give credit and appreciation to others.

At other times, honor needs to be modeled so others can observe it in action. While God has used many people to teach me the meaning of honor, one person stands out. He is my close friend and the executive pastor of the church where I serve as senior pastor. His name is Ron.

Ron makes it clear to everyone he meets, his job is to serve me and the vision God has given me. Over the years he has been offered many opportunities for promotion or to pastor his own church. With each request, his reply was always, "Thank you, but I know where God has called me to serve. I am to serve my senior pastor."

Several times I have asked Ron why he felt the way he did, and why he refused offers to become senior pastor of his own church. His answer has always been the same, "You are closer to me than a brother. I love to serve with you and believe in the vision God has given you. You've won my heart."

I believe that a defining moment in our relationship came many years ago when Ron was invited to become senior pastor of a large church in our city. When he broke the news, I think he was expecting a negative response from me. Instead, I reassured him, "You have my total support. Yes, I will miss you, but I am more concerned that you fulfil God's call on your life. I will always be your friend and be there to support you."

As it turned out, after a series of meetings with the new church, Ron felt God's leading to remain at Churchlands. Since that time, he has become my closest colleague. I trust him implicitly. He is unswerving in his loyalty, confidentiality and support, both in public and private. Without him at my side, I would be unable to fulfil God's call on my life.

God has used my colleague to illustrate what it means to honor another human being. He honors me above himself. He constantly encourages me and is willing to speak the truth in love when I need it.

The importance of honor is reinforced as we do it. As the practice of honoring others becomes the norm rather than the exception, others catch on and begin to behave in a similar way. But the fact is that someone has to take the initiative and begin modeling honor for this to happen.

What I've seen modeled by Ron, I am beginning to see other leaders put into practice. Perhaps I am the best example of this transition. Ron's example has touched my heart and reminded me of the importance of honor. All the years of self-preservation and holding back have given way to an incredible desire to be part of helping others succeed. Through the honor of a colleague, God is turning my heart to my spiritual children. And as a result, their hearts are being turned back to me.

The Greek word for love, *agape*, means the ability to do everything you can to help another person become the greatest of what they can be. In 1 Corinthians 13:4–7, Paul expands on the attributes of *agape*.

> Love is patient, love is kind. It does not envy, it does not boast, it is not proud. It is not rude, it is not self-seeking, it is not easily angered, it keeps no record of wrongs. Love rejoices with the truth. It always protects, always trusts, always hopes, always perseveres.

Loving relationships form the foundation of a culture of honor. To honor someone is to *love* them in a way that lifts them to become more like Jesus. True honor is not verbal stroking; it is protecting, trusting, hoping and persevering in whatever it takes to achieve God's highest for another person.

TRUE HONOR IS NOT VERBAL STROKING.

Jesus said that all men would know we were his disciples by our love for each other.[11] As Christians embody this love, two things will happen: our critics will be silenced and the world will be drawn toward us.

THE NEED FOR HONOR IN THE CHURCH

Honor is a rare commodity in the church. Often people are quick to criticize or dishonor others if their behavior is challenged or a decision is made that they misunderstand or disagree with. Many of us are unaware of the sacrifices others continually make for our benefit behind the scenes.

Insensitivity and ingratitude lie at the heart of the culture of dishonor that thrives in many churches. They are symptoms of the frog in the kettle—worldly selfishness and self-centeredness that have gone unchallenged. It's just too easy to believe the worst of people than to believe for the best. Galatians 5:15 warns us that if we keep on biting and devouring each other, we'll end up destroying each other. The enemy may load the bullets, but we end up firing the gun.

Division rises from a culture of dishonor. In the ministry, I have observed the enemy's strategy many times over the years. He tries to find a foothold in the shadows of innuendo, the bitterness of gossip, or jealousy and envy. Wherever there is a gap in communication or relationship, there the enemy will focus his attack.

I discovered this truth many years ago when two congregational groups I pastored became so unhappy with each other that a church split occurred. One group favored a more traditional service and the other a more evangelistic and contemporary form. I had worked for several years to move the church on to a more evangelistic footing.

In hindsight, the plan ultimately split the church because our focus was more on programs than relationships. I must take much of the responsibility for this. I had become very frustrated with the traditional group. A number of new and progressively minded people had come into the church, and so I made the choice to work with those who shared my vision. While my vision was biblical and the majority supported change, I still managed to alienate many members.

I was not always honest because I felt intimidated and wanted to avoid confrontation. In the end, I cannot blame my intimidation on anyone else. This experience has taught me that unity often hangs by a slender thread. The congregation had come to this point because I had failed to be honest and present my views wisely and with respect. I had come across in a biased and uncompromising way. While I felt justified with our cause, and had majority support, I did not really honor the views of my critics.

I had been guilty of verbal flattery. Superficial honor is called flattery. Flattery is short-lived and conditional. It is essentially words that never become deeds. True honor involves loving actions as well as words. God wants us to honor others even when we have nothing to gain from it. He wants honor to be expressed between all the generations within the church.

Whether these members would ultimately have moved forward, no one knows. What I faced was an angry group of dissenters who would go on to divide again and turn on each other. I did little to foster a culture of honor. I have learned that it's not enough to plan the right programs; we must also foster honest relationship.

The church must become desperate to see right relationships flourish. We all know that no one is perfect. If we wait till people do all the right things or make all the right decisions, we will never honor them. Honor is not based on someone else's perfection. It is based on the order that our heavenly Father has established.

> HONOR IS NOT BASED ON SOMEONE ELSE'S PERFECTION.

God stated His intentions in the Ten Commandments. The fifth commandment tells us, "Honor your father and mother, so that you may live long in the land the Lord your God is giving you."[12] This is a command that results in a blessing or curse, depending on whether we obey or disobey it. Honor brings blessing, dishonor brings a curse.

The Lord has given us parents to teach us the meaning of honor. If our parents fail in this task, we are nevertheless to honor them to the best of our ability. God did not say to honor our father and mother ONLY if we think they deserve it. Unfortunately, honor has become a conditional accolade in our society.

THE FOUNDATION OF EMPOWERING RELATIONSHIPS

Submission and respect enable us to form empowering relationships. When we honor someone, we give them respect and submit our agenda to what will bring blessing in their lives. In

Ephesians 5:21 Paul challenged the believers to submit to one another out of reverence for Christ.

Submission means to get underneath and push upward. We have an attitude of submission if we are willing to serve another's mission and do all we can to make them successful. It's all about selfless serving. When people realize that another person has gone to great lengths to serve or bless them, it softens their hearts. Jesus highlights the importance of submissive servanthood in Matthew 20:25–28:

> Jesus called them together and said, "You know that the rulers of the Gentiles lord it over them, and their high officials exercise authority over them. Not so with you. Instead, whoever wants to become great among you must be your servant, and whoever wants to be first must be your slave—just as the Son of Man did not come to be served, but to serve, and to give his life as a ransom for many."

He went on to say in John 13:34–35, "A new command I give you: Love one another. As I have loved you, so you must love one another. By this all men will know that you are my disciples, if you love one another."

Institutional thinking and impersonal relationships have become the culture of many congregations. In time, this can change if we become committed to serving and honoring one another. When caring, honor and submission are cherished and become our lifestyle, a culture is formed and passed to the next generation.

Honor and submission strengthen the witness of the church to the world. Dishonor and independence project a message to non-Christians that faith is irrelevant and outdated. Before the world will embrace the gospel, it needs to see love, honor and submission being practised within the body of Christ. This was undoubtedly one of the reasons why the church in Acts 2 grew so rapidly.

RESTORING HONOR

To restore honor to the church, God is doing two things: pouring out His grace and raising up apostles and apostolic teams.

Grace, we recall, is the desire and power to do God's will. It is an amazing gift. We can't earn it. Neither can we receive it without God's permission. Without grace we can do very little to please God and almost nothing to fulfil His will. God's grace enables us to honor one another above ourselves, be servants, and submit to and love one another.

God is restoring apostolic ministry to establish honor in the church. The heart of an apostle is the heart of a spiritual father or mother. Ephesians 4:14–15 reveals that apostolic ministry brings a reality to the church when:

> We will no longer be infants, tossed back and forth by the waves, and blown here and there by every wind of teaching and by the cunning and craftiness of men in their deceitful scheming. Instead, speaking the truth in love, we will in all things grow up into him who is the Head, that is, Christ.

Apostles have an anointing to establish the church in proper relationships. The term *apostolic* refers to the ministry of apostles but also includes teams of five-fold ministries, prophets, evangelists, pastors and teachers working in cooperation, "to prepare God's people for works of service, until we reach unity in the faith, and become mature."[6]

Apostles and prophets have a special grace to release relationship and succession. When they work together it results in a synergy that strengthens every aspect of church life. As the church embraces apostles and prophets, we will see an increase in wisdom, revelation and power. Ephesians 2:19–20 speaks of the key role of apostles and prophets:

> Consequently, you are no longer foreigners and aliens, but fellow citizens with God's people and members of God's household, built on the foundation of the apostles and

prophets, with Christ Jesus himself as the chief corner-stone.

While the foundation is always based on the work of Jesus, apostles and prophets bring a grace to establish the church in love and faith. As God's relational grace increases, a culture of honor and spiritual succession will gradually develop.

This will not happen overnight but may take several generations. In the meantime, we must pass on the baton of learning to honor others, particularly those in positions of spiritual and secular authority. What we sow today in honor will be reaped by our descendants in the emergence of true spiritual sons and daughters.

CHAPTER FIVE—REALITY CHECK

- God has given us parents to teach us the meaning of honor. How easy or difficult has it been for you to learn this from your parents?

- Honor is based on respect and submission. Given this definition, who can you say that you honor? Why is this so?

- What are your experiences of unity and disunity in life, in the church, and in your family?

CHAPTER SIX

GROWING IN A SPIRIT OF SONSHIP

And the things you have heard me say in the presence of many witnesses entrust to reliable men who will also be qualified to teach others. —2 Timothy 2:2

To have a spirit of sonship is to put yourself underneath another's mission and do all you can to make them successful, knowing that as a son or daughter, there is an inheritance that lies ahead. —Jack Frost

As mutual honor grows in God's house, true sons and daughters begin to emerge who have a heart for the things that please the Lord. Only God can match fathers to sons, and mothers to daughters. But how do we know who to work alongside? We need spiritual discernment. If we are faithful in building into the right sons and daughters, and they learn to be faithful, eventually they too will grow in wisdom and authority to become spiritual fathers and mothers. This is how the line of spiritual succession continues.

I began my life as a son in the house of my father and mother. My father was a meat salesman. Five days a week he would get up before sunrise and drive a meat delivery truck, taking orders and supplying his customers with everything from sides of beef to boxes of bacon. Once in a while, Dad would take me with him to help out.

Arriving at the first stop, I would listen as Dad took the order. I would help him by carrying boxes and putting them in the walk-in freezer. Then we'd stop somewhere, often on the side of a country road, to eat sandwiches and talk. I didn't get paid for helping my dad, I just wanted to be with him and it made me feel good to help him out in a small way.

As I got older, I began to realize things around the house that needed to be painted or repaired. In those days we often couldn't afford to pay a handyman, so I learned to repair small items, apply wallpaper, and even to install a suspended ceiling. Again, the thought of being paid never crossed my mind; I was happy to help out in the house where I lived and grew up.

This pattern of serving in the house of others was repeated in several jobs I had as a student, and continued when I eventually became an ordained minister. All of them were opportunities for me to learn faithfulness.

My greatest challenge as a spiritual son came when John Wimber asked me to help him establish Vineyard churches in Australia. I undertook this task with enthusiasm and believed, with God's help, I could accomplish the task. I remained in that role for four years, until his death in 1997.

In seeking God and some of my closest friends, I felt that God was opening a new door for me in ministry. I had a stirring to attempt something that I had never done before, to establish an international network of ministries throughout the Southern Hemisphere. I put some thoughts on paper and circulated them to some of my colleagues in other parts of the world. They were encouraging to me, but I knew the final decision was in my hands.

When it comes to taking risks and attempting new things, the final decision is always in your court. Others cannot make the decision for you; it has to be between you and God. I am so glad I said yes to starting Southern Cross. God has blessed it immensely and it has grown to include many churches and leaders on four continents.

The point is, I could not be involved in my current work until I had first learned to serve **faithfully** in the houses of other men and women. This is one of God's principles that I have seen repeatedly in the ministry. If we are faithful with little, then the Lord will put us in charge of much.[13]

ELIJAH AND ELISHA

I never tire of reading the story of Elijah and Elisha. Both had incredible ministries, yet one successfully passed his mantle and the other failed. What was the difference? The answer is simple. Elijah passed his mantle to a spiritual son. Elisha chose a man not worthy of his trust.

Elisha followed Elijah wherever he went. Sons should always chase spiritual fathers, not the other way around! His heart was to please Elijah. He had a spirit of sonship. Because Elisha served as a son, God permitted him to inherit a double portion of Elijah's anointing.

In contrast, Elisha selected Gehazi as his understudy. On the surface, Gehazi showed promise, but his heart concealed the darkness of dishonesty and cunning. Gehazi failed to serve Elisha as a son. Consequently, he failed God's school of character.

Not everyone who seeks to serve God has learned how to serve faithfully. Over the years I have met many men and women who will only serve if there's something in it for them. They serve conditionally and when they are tested or challenged, their true hearts are revealed.

There are two kinds of attitude we can develop in ministry: that of a son or of an orphan. If we are to successfully pass our baton to the next generation, we must build into men and women who are spiritual sons and daughters. We need to be careful in choosing who will inherit our mantle.

EXPOSING THE ORPHAN SPIRIT

The term *orphan spirit* is used to describe an attitude or spirit of self-preservation, independence, and manipulation. Many people who evidence an *orphan spirit* are not, in fact, biological orphans. By using this term I do not wish to ridicule or devalue people who have lost their parents. Orphans are very precious to God. I use the term to illustrate a destructive pattern of behavior that is very common both inside and outside the church. The orphan spirit is very independent and self-centered.

Orphans, because of separation from their biological parents, have been deprived of life's most formative relationships. Perceiving that they have missed out and have no inheritance feeds a spirit of self-preservation and the need to fend for themselves. Self-preservation fuels attitudes of deep insecurity, extreme independence, mistrust of authority, and a compulsion to achieve.

There are many in ministry today who are deeply insecure and independent. They will only play on a team if they can lead it. They have no interest in building into others beyond the point to which it will benefit them directly. Consequently, they build walls around their ministries to protect themselves against outside threats.

It is possible to minister God's healing to a person having an independent spirit, but they will need to humble themselves and genuinely repent. I have found that self-preservation is a very difficult spirit to break in the short term. It often requires time and a high degree of accountability by the person concerned. A person with an orphan spirit can cause great damage or division to a ministry if placed in leadership without the fruit of repentance being evident.

God loves all people, including those who for whatever reason are insecure and self-centered. The Lord may give you a heart for a person with an orphan perspective, and that is good. Before making a commitment to become their spiritual father or mother, you are wise to seek counsel and assistance in dealing with the root of their insecurity.

SPIRITUAL SONS AND DAUGHTERS

The goal of a spiritual parent is to build into the men and women who God is leading you to. This may be one person or half a dozen. The issue isn't how many, but who? If we choose those who God has already chosen, our chances of passing the baton effectively increase.

True spiritual sons and daughters are content to be in relationship and serve without expectation of reward or recognition. They trust that God has led them into relationship with you. They know that in due time God will promote them to the place where they are called to be. Consequently, they are people who can be built into with confidence, knowing that the investment of our time will bear fruit.

Sons and daughters are nurtured through the security of safe and benevolent relationships. Knowing that we are valued and accepted, no matter what, frees us from the need of self-preservation. The hope of an inheritance promotes trust and a generous heart. True sons and daughters have no need to manipulate others. The kindness modeled by their fathers and mothers feeds a heart attitude of submission—the willingness to be subject to another's mission.

Jesus modeled a heart of submission by doing only what He saw the Father doing.[14] His mission was simply to do the will of the Father. Sons are secure in relationships. They know that an inheritance lies ahead if they are faithful. Chuck Clayton provides a helpful contrast between the attitude of sons and orphans (see extra material).[15]

The Heart of a Son	The Heart of an Orphan
Sons build the house.	Orphans serve in the house out of duty, doing only what they have to.
Sons hold the father's vision as their own and seek to accomplish it.	Orphans serve only the parts of the vision that they like.
Sons speak by using family language: we—our—us—one another.	Orphans use individual terminology: me—my—I—mine.
Sons bond newcomers into the family.	Orphans gather new people to themselves.
Sons have a stake in the family business, knowing they have an inheritance.	Orphans look for sundown and a paycheck.
Sons stay put under fire.	Orphans look for greener pastures.

Identifying spiritual sons and daughters

As a leader, one of the tasks I find most challenging is to choose the right person for a job. When Jesus selected His disciples, He was looking for men who would become spiritual sons and would last the distance. We need discernment in identifying sons and daughters. Some who I thought were sons were actually very good actors and clever at telling me what I wanted to hear. To choose wisely we need to develop spiritual eyes that look beyond natural potential and abilities.

I have always found Bill Hybels' counsel in *Courageous Leadership*[16] helpful in choosing an employee or colleague to work with. He speaks of three qualities to look for: character, competence and chemistry. These same qualities help us identify sons and daughters.

Character is high on my list of considerations. Does the person I'm considering building into have good character? Character, we recall, is where Gehazi fell short of the mark.

What do we mean by character? What do we look for? I look for loyalty, honesty, humility, reliability, a good work ethic, and openness to correction. If a person possesses these qualities, they most likely have certain spiritual disciplines, like prayer and generosity, in place. Character is important because it indicates a willingness to live a lifestyle congruent with God's Word.

Ultimately, character is revealed on the journey of life. People can put on a façade for a while, and if they're clever, even keep their true nature hidden from you. Eventually, though, the toothpaste tube gets squeezed, and what's inside comes out!

Competence, or the skills people possess, is not as high on my list of prerequisites. Spiritual sons and daughters often start out awkward in spiritual things, but improve with time and experience. Competence can be developed if a person has the passion to learn and opportunities to be taught and gain experience.

It is important in learning a skill that a person has a degree of aptitude, or ability to grasp the basic concepts required for a task. Working with a person who constantly needs prodding is not a good investment of our time.

Chemistry is essential in determining who we will build into. Chemistry refers to natural attraction between two people. Ask yourself: Do I really enjoy this person's company? Do we connect? Do I have a heart for this person, and they for me? Could I see this person as a long-term friend?

While often overlooked, chemistry is an important consideration in selecting sons and daughters. We naturally relate to some people more easily than others, so I look for sons and daughters who are team players. The ability to work and get along with others, especially those we normally wouldn't relate to, is an important people skill.

Looking beneath the surface

After examining the exterior, I always ask what the Holy Spirit is saying about a prospective son or daughter. This requires careful prayer, listening to God and asking some key questions.

- What impression is the Holy Spirit giving me about this person? Are there words of knowledge that the Spirit is revealing?

- What do I perceive to be God's call on their life?

- Are they of the same spirit or do they have a different attitude, worldview, and motivation from myself?

- Do I perceive in them a call to the five-fold ministry? (apostle, prophet, evangelist, pastor, and teacher)

Taking time to wait on God, and not rushing into things, dramatically increases our chances of selecting wisely. I constantly remind myself, "Man looks at the outward appearance, but the Lord looks at the heart."[17] Elijah chose wisely and Elisha chose poorly. When it comes to passing on the baton, only true sons and daughters will last the distance and pass on their baton to others.

Receiving the baton

Before we can pass the baton, we must first learn what it means to receive one. For me this has meant two things:

- seeing the importance of what the person has to impart to me; and

- being humble and teachable enough to allow someone to teach me.

I have always had a great respect for my spiritual mentors. I could see that they had been through experiences that I had yet to go through. They had paid a price to learn the lessons of life that I stood to gain from for a fraction of the cost.

I believe you can learn something from anyone who crosses our path. Great pearls of wisdom are all around us for the taking, but we need to always be on the lookout for such gems, even when they come from the mouths of those who do not have a personal relationship with the Lord.

One day I had the privilege of sitting next to a former Prime Minister of Australia on the five-hour flight between Sydney and Perth. Although this man was an avowed agnostic, I probed him and asked, "What is the greatest leadership lesson you have ever learned?" He replied, "I survived many challenges to my leadership because I took the time to listen to those who had concerns. Even if I had to make a decision that went against their point of view, they didn't oppose me, because they knew they'd had a fair hearing."

I learned a lot in those five hours. Everyone has something of value to teach us, but we need to grasp the opportunities when they present themselves.

Second, we need to be humble and teachable. At times we will encounter teachers whose attitude or appearance will obscure the value of what they are saying. This is when we need humility and to remain teachable.

> YOU CAN'T TAKE SOMEONE WHERE YOU YOURSELF HAVE NOT BEEN.

I hold a doctorate degree from an American seminary which required many years of arduous study and writing. The more I have learned formally, the more I desire to be teachable. I have vowed to always remain open to correction and learning new things. This openness has enabled me to glean from fields where I did not sow.

Finally, to fully receive a baton as a son, you must desire to apply those lessons that will enhance your life and make you more effective. Knowledge is of little value unless it is used to improve your life. I once asked a great evangelist if he had any regrets about his ministry. He simply said, "I wish I had spent more time with my kids as they were growing up."

I can relate to that regret. It is so easy to follow one's career, and yet neglect those closest to us. The pull of task over relationship is very strong. We need to balance the scales in favor of time spent with our loved ones.

When it comes to passing on the baton, God has a guideline. As we learn to serve faithfully as sons and daughters, the Lord will entrust us with more. Only through faithful serving, submission and humility can we be shaped and grow in the wisdom and the character of Christ.

Remember, you can't take someone where you yourself have not been.

Chapter Six—Reality Check

- How would you describe the difference between a spiritual son and a person who demonstrates an orphan spirit?

- In reference to Chuck Clayton's list, what are the qualities that best express you and how you view life? What are the areas you need to work on? (see extra material)

- Do you know anyone who is a potential spiritual son or daughter? How would you evaluate them in terms of character, competence and chemistry?

CHAPTER SEVEN

BECOMING A
SPIRITUAL PARENT

Even though you have ten thousand guardians in Christ, you do not have many fathers, for in Christ Jesus I became your father through the gospel. Therefore I urge you to imitate me.

—1 Corinthians 4:15–16

The challenge for every leader is to make their ceiling become the ground floor for the next generation. We need to build a platform that others can stand on to take our work where we did not have the time to take it. The world is full of mantles that have been lost and need to be repossessed.

—Bill Johnson

God's heart is that spiritual fathers and mothers be multiplied and released throughout the body of Christ. For most, the thought of becoming a spiritual parent is unnerving. In this chapter, we examine the transition from sonship to fatherhood. While there is no set path to becoming a spiritual parent, eventually we must develop in three areas: possessing the heart of a father, developing in the role of a father, and raising children who share our desire to pass the baton.

When I was growing up little was said about the need for spiritual fathers and mothers. Instead, our church focused on discipleship programs, Bible studies, small groups, and youth activities as the means of building into sons and daughters. The prevailing strategy seemed to be that if kids were educated in Sunday school and went through confirmation class, then they would probably grow up to be good church members.

Being a good Christian was defined in terms of church membership and participating in the life of a local congregation. The focus, unfortunately, was more on outward appearance and works than on growing in Christlikeness. This is institutional thinking.

FOR TOO LONG WE HAVE TRIED TO MASS PRODUCE MATURE CHRISTIANS.

I'm not saying we should throw out involvement in the local church or Bible study. While it is essential to be involved in a local church and knowledgeable in the Bible and issues of our faith, there is an aspect of spiritual growth that institutional Christianity has often failed to grasp: the significance of one-on-one empowering relationships.

There is a saying: "The kingdom of God is built one person at a time." For too long we have tried to mass produce mature Christians. Like making a cake, we have thought if we add the right ingredients, stir the mixture and put it in the oven, then presto, out comes a mature Christian. Unfortunately, making disciples is not that simple.

Another wrong assumption we have embraced is that parents are the only ones to raise their children spiritually. It has often been assumed that if your parents knew the Lord, then they would naturally pass on their faith to their children.

The fact is, while parents play a crucial role in their children coming to faith, it is often people outside of the immediate family who significantly build into our children and become role models and mentors of faith. Spiritual parents play an essential role in discipleship.

THE VALUE OF SPIRITUAL PARENTS

The value of having spiritual parents has been borne out in my life and the lives of many around me. My first spiritual parents, Don and Pat, came into my life when I was nineteen. I had just made a recommitment to Christ and wanted to really get serious with God. Following my decision, I was taken under the wing by this couple, who oversaw a ministry at a local coffee house. They built into about a dozen regulars, mainly single young adults, through study groups and on weekends.

Don and Pat opened my heart to God's Word. I loved the short-term studies of books by such authors as Dennis and Rita Bennett, Hal Lindsay, and Watchman Nee. It was also great to interact with other growing Christians in an informal coffee house setting. What made this experience different from being part of a Christian youth group, however, was that I was singled out by Don and Pat for individual attention. They took time to hear my heartbeat and made one-on-one time for me.

After approximately nine months, Don and Pat accepted an invitation to become pastors at a church in another state. I was sad to see my first spiritual parents go, but knew it was a wonderful opportunity for them and that God was in it. I am happy to say that we still keep in touch and the Lord uses them to build into my life.

There was something very special about this relationship that I have always held on to. God brought a spiritual father and mother into my life when I needed them most. They built my confidence and confirmed God's call on my life. Without them, I think my life might have taken a very different course.

To continue with the story, after Don and Pat moved, I embarked on a path toward becoming a minister in the denomination of my home church. Soon I was pastoring a church on weekends and learning how to preach, lead small groups and visit the members. Most of these skills were learned on my own, by trial and error, without having a spiritual father or mother who I could relate to. Like many of my colleagues, I became very independent and self-sufficient in my approach to ministry.

I WAS…GOOD AT ORGANIZING THINGS, YET I KNEW SOMETHING WAS MISSING.

For twenty-five years, the thought of being or needing a spiritual father rarely crossed my mind. While I had some great relationships with many leaders, it didn't occur to me to build into anybody one-on-one.

I attended lots of seminars and conferences on leadership, spent time building into our staff, and even established an international network of ministries. I was a producer and good at organizing things, yet I knew something was missing. That something was the Father's heart for people.

My path toward becoming a spiritual father started with a revelation of God's heart for people. The Lord began speaking to me through a number of the most incredible circumstances about Malachi 4 and the necessity of "turning the hearts of the fathers to the children, and the children to the fathers." I came to understand that God's plan is to return the church to its relational foundations, where spiritual fathers and mothers turn their hearts to sons and daughters. It's amazing how one *rhema* word begins to open a panacea of revelation that can change our perspective!

God showed me that relationship is the heart of revival. Often we see revival as some mystical intervention of God where people are swept up into a frenzy of religious activity. God wants revival to be more than a flash in the pan or something short-lived; He wants it to be an ongoing reality within the life of the church, preserved and continuing right up to the time of Jesus' second coming. For this to happen, we need a change of heart.

THE FATHER'S HEART

According to Malachi 4, the hearts of the fathers **must** be turned to the children. It took God years to turn my heart. My focus in ministry was on my career, my accomplishment. I became distracted, self-satisfied and passive. To become spiritual fathers and mothers, the focus needs to shift from our perspective to God's.

God's grace enables us to see the hearts and lives of young people in a new way. Once upon a time, I believe the Lord looked at me and said, "That young man has potential. I'm going to put into motion a chain of events that will enable Him to be my son and servant." The Lord now enables me to see younger men and women in this way. I want to do all that I can to help them get a good start toward God's destiny.

God's perspective also helps us look beyond character flaws, awkwardness and immaturity. God has a way of shifting our gaze to recognize the potential in our sons and daughters. Rather than having a mentality of correction, the Lord enables us to focus on developing the good things He has started in the lives of others.

In considering how to better reflect the Father's heart, I take a cue from Romans 12:9–13:

> Love must be sincere. Hate what is evil; cling to what is good. Be devoted to one another in brotherly love. Honor one another above yourselves. Never be lacking in zeal, but keep your spiritual fervor, serving the Lord. Be joyful in hope, patient in affliction, faithful in prayer. Share with God's people who are in need. Practice hospitality.

Spiritual fathers and mothers need to model God's love in all situations. This love must be sincere, loyal, brotherly, zealous, joyful, patient, faithful, generous, and hospitable. We must come to the realization that, because God has been so good to us, we should seek to bless and build into the lives of others.

When God increases His grace, we see opportunities like never before to build into others. We discover a joy greater than personal accomplishment; it is the satisfaction of seeing another person become the greatest of what they can be for God.

MY GREATEST JOY IS TO SEE OTHERS SUCCEED.

I have come to see myself as one who builds bridges between the generations. Recently I received a prophetic word indicating that, like Joseph, I was a man who carried the dreams of others in my heart. This describes me to a tee! Now, my greatest joy is to see others succeed.

When you take a younger man or woman under your wing, you learn how to carry the dreams of others in your heart. You are learning to love others as you love yourself. In reality, you are taking the Word of God into your heart and allowing others to benefit from lessons it took you years to learn.

In other words, we want others to have a head start—for our ceiling to become the ground floor for the next generation. Building relationships is what turns the hearts of the children back to the fathers.

THE FOUR ROLES OF SPIRITUAL PARENTS

Spiritual parenting combines a loving attitude with action. Our activity as fathers and mothers is seen in four roles that reflect God's love. God's fatherly heart is revealed through *mentoring*. His desire to be our friend and encourager is seen in *coaching*. *Sponsoring* reveals His wish to be the author and finisher of our faith. The Father sent Jesus to model His nature and set an *example* for us to follow.

MENTORING

Mentors are people *who have been* where we want to go. Because of extensive experience in their field, mentors have confidence and certainty. This attracts people who want advice. A mentor leads from the top and is good at giving answers and telling people how to accomplish their goals or overcome an obstacle.

When Paul wrote the pastoral letters of First and Second Timothy, he was writing as a mentor to his spiritual son. His letters are brimming with instruction on a variety of issues Timothy faced in ministry. Mentors are both directive and practical. Their focus is on "how to." They have an ability to take people through systematic steps to reach a desired outcome.

COACHING

Unlike mentors, coaches get beside a leader and ask strategic questions that help the person to come up with their own solution. Coaches have developed the ability to listen carefully before they speak. They also hold their protégés accountable for achieving pre-determined goals.

We all need to set goals, but they must be realistic and appropriate. Once goals are set, coaches refrain from telling people what to do. Instead, they help others discover answers within themselves. This can be quite frustrating for people who want to be given instructions! A good coach allows this tension to grow until his charge gets the point and begins to take initiative. Coaches allow others to grow by providing hands-on experience and allowing people to learn from their mistakes.

Barnabas was a great coach. His name means *son of encouragement*. In Acts 11:25–26 we read, "Then Barnabas went to Tarsus to look for Saul, and when he found him, he brought him to Antioch. For a whole year Barnabas and Saul met with the church and taught great numbers of people."

Barnabas coached Saul and for a year they ministered side by side in Antioch. Traveling together, they took the gospel to new frontiers and established a pattern of missionary expansion that Paul would later develop. Good coaches have an ability to multiply and release leaders who reproduce themselves.

Colin Noyes defines coaching as, "a process of coming alongside a person or team and helping them discover God's agenda for their life and ministry. This means cooperating with the Holy Spirit to see that agenda become a reality." He sees coaching as a process of five R's.[18]

- **Relating** to establish a coaching relationship and agenda;

- **Reflecting** to discover and explore key issues;

- **Refocusing** to determine priorities and action steps;

- **Resourcing** to provide support and encouragement; and

- **Reviewing** to evaluate, celebrate progress, and revise as necessary.

SPONSORING

Sponsors are people who take us out of our comfort zone. They have an innate ability to see potential and push others forward. Jesus did this in Luke 10 when he sent seventy-two of his disciples out in pairs, "Go! I am sending you like lambs among wolves."[19]

Jesus was pushing his protégés to sink or swim! Sometimes that's the only way. A good sponsor takes people to the precipice when they will not go willingly. I thank God for those who gave me a push when I needed it. One such time for me was my first attempt at preaching.

Shortly after my spiritual parents were established in their new church, they invited me to preach at their evening service. They knew I had never preached before. What they didn't know was that I was both honored and terrified at the prospect.

When I finally stood before their congregation of two hundred, my heart lodged in my throat. I don't remember the message at all. At the end I simply sat down, feeling a great sense of relief at having faced my fears and survived!

I learned a big lesson that day. God lives in trees. We meet God when we go out on limbs. Sponsors push us from our comfort zones and lift us to a higher level.

WE MEET GOD WHEN WE GO OUT ON LIMBS.

BEING AN EXAMPLE

Some of life's most important lessons are learned simply by observation. Spiritual parents model behavior that others watch and use as a guide for their lives. This places on us the responsibility to practice what we preach.

People often **become** what they see in their leaders. Whenever I visit a church, I can usually tell what the pastor is like just by meeting a few church members. If a pastor is friendly, so are the people. If he or she is very businesslike, they will be as well. I am amazed that some people even copy their leader's hairstyle, clothing, or the way they walk! Leaders, by their example, set a pattern for others to follow.

Paul exhorted Timothy, "What you heard from me, keep as the pattern of sound teaching, with faith and love in Christ Jesus."[20] Paul was confident that he set a good example. Are we confident in the way we model Christ? Can we honestly say to our spiritual kids, "Imitate me as I imitate Christ?"

Good spiritual parents model integrity. They are secure enough to admit their failures. They are transparent and admit that they walk with a limp. Honesty combines with humility in giving God and others credit for their successes.

IMPARTING A DESIRE FOR SPIRITUAL SUCCESSION

So far we have seen that a good spiritual parent has God's heart perspective of people. This heart is expressed through the skills of mentoring, coaching, sponsoring, and being an example. There remains one further important consideration for fathers and mothers: imparting to others the desire to one day pass the baton to their children.

Numerous examples in the Bible warn that a person being a great servant of the Lord is no guarantee of leaving a legacy. Joshua and Elisha failed in passing on the baton to their successors. We need to take steps to ensure that our sons and daughters pass the test. I believe we can do this in three ways: reinforce, repeat and reinvent.

We **reinforce** the need for succession in two ways: by reminding our sons and daughters of its importance and by providing opportunities to learn through hands-on experience. We must constantly remind our sons and daughters of the importance of the task and the need to have both a Barnabas and Timothy in our lives at all times. Barnabas is someone who builds into us, and Timothy is someone we are building into.

People learn best by doing. Sons and daughters should be encouraged early to choose a protégé and repeat the process. This reinforces confidence and establishes a multiplication pattern in their lives.

Repeating the process means continually taking new people under our wing. Repetition is an important part of developing habits and a lifestyle. Our sons and daughters need to multiply their involvements in empowering relationships—multiplication establishes a culture of succession.

Finally, we occasionally need to **reinvent** ourselves and how we relate to others. To reinvent is to change with the times and seek to be more relevant and a better communicator. The preaching style I learned in seminary is no longer effective in communicating with many young people. We need to reinvent ourselves to be current and relevant to the people we are seeking to form in Christlikeness.

The gospel message is timeless, but how we present it needs to be relevant. It is so important for us to encourage our sons and daughters in the freedom to keep up with the times and be willing to change.

The journey of becoming a spiritual parent begins with a single step. The first step is to say yes to God and make ourselves available to Him. The second step is to seek out spiritual sons and daughters. And finally, we attempt to pass on what God has given us in a way that can be passed successively on to others.

In the final part of the book, we look at developing a strategy for encouraging loving, empowering relationships in order to fulfil the Great Commission.

CHAPTER SEVEN—REALITY CHECK

- What does it mean to make your ceiling the ground floor of the next generation?

- Consider the mentors, coaches, sponsors and those who have been an example in your life. What lessons have you learned from them that could be passed to others?

- Of the four roles of a spiritual parent, what is your strongest area? Which is your weakest?

PART THREE

DEVELOPING
A STRATEGY

But you will receive power when the Holy Spirit comes upon you; and you will be my witnesses in Jerusalem, and in Judea and Samaria, and to the ends of the earth.

—Acts 1:8

A CHANGE
OF HEART

When he was at the table with them, he took bread, gave
thanks, broke it and began to give it to them. Then their
eyes were opened and they recognized him, and he disappeared from their sight. They asked each other "Were not
our hearts burning within us while he talked with us on the
road and opened the Scriptures to us?"

—Luke 24:30–32

Happiness is a butterfly, which, when pursued, is always
just beyond your grasp, but which, if you will sit down
quietly, may alight upon you.

—Nathaniel Hawthorne

*In these final chapters, we look at developing a strategy for passing on the
baton in the local church. There is no single strategy that works for everyone.
No magic formula for us to use. Each of us must seek the Lord for direction.
Strategy is birthed when Jesus reveals His Word to us and implants His vision*

of passing on the baton in our hearts. As God's heart for the next generation is revealed to us, our hearts as parents are turned toward the children.

It takes only a small amount of God's revelation to totally change your life. Hearing directly from the Lord sharpens our focus and fires our passion to pursue His will. Look at Saul on the road to Damascus.[21] When God reveals something to you, He has a very good reason for doing so. He is recruiting you for a mission.

On a sunny autumn day nearly twenty years ago, I felt led to spend time praying at a war memorial that sits on a high vantage point overlooking our city, Perth. From this high place, I marveled at the panoramic view of the entire city sprawling in every direction.

In a split second the Lord spoke a word into my spirit that changed my heart for the city. He said, "I will give this entire city and all that you see into the hands of my people, IF they will learn to live in unity."

Within weeks of this revelation, I received part two of the vision. It happened as I was driving into the parking lot of a church across the city, where I had been invited to speak at the Sunday evening service. The church sits on land next to a power transmission corridor. Near the church are several mammoth power pylons and the one nearest the church caught my attention. Each pylon carried three high voltage power cables that sagged toward the ground in the gap between them.

Then the Lord spoke to me again, "I will raise seven power pylons within the city. These pylons represent churches whose pastors will have a heart for one another. These churches will form a ring of unity, and churches throughout the city will reach up and grasp the sagging wires that hang between them."

I was ecstatic that God would reveal such a thing to me! Because the visions were so vivid, they made a deep and lasting impression. For nearly two decades I have shared this vision with many people, and I know God has used it to draw the body of Christ closer together.

But its ultimate fulfillment is yet to come. Relationship is the basis of trust. I know God has told me to build bridges of relationship between pastors, not only in our city, but throughout the Southern Hemisphere. God has given me a boundary stone to work within.

THE ROAD TO EMMAUS

Consider the disciples on the road to Emmaus. They had been faithful, deeply loved their Lord, and yet seemed unaware of the Father's purposes in Jesus' death and resurrection. Sometimes we can be so caught up in the culture of church that we miss hearing the heartbeat of God for our generation. We are, in a general sense, committed to Christ, but lack the passion that drives us to go out on limbs of faith.

Vision snaps us out of our lethargy. When the two disciples met up with a stranger on the road to Emmaus, they invited their newfound friend to join them for dinner, and in a moment their lives were changed forever. In the breaking of bread, their eyes were opened and they recognized Jesus! Wow, what a shock! He immediately disappeared from their sight, but that didn't really matter.

VISION SNAPS US OUT OF OUR LETHARGY.

In that split second, two men's lives were changed. "Were not our hearts burning within us while he talked with us on the road and opened the Scriptures to us?"[22] It took a personal encounter with the risen Lord to turn these otherwise average guys into agents of change. The same must happen to each of us.

Today's churches are filled with men and women on the road to Emmaus; they are faithful and committed to their congregations and to God's work. But something is often missing, and that something is passion.

Nothing stirs passion more than when God reveals your purpose for being on this earth and what a difference your life can make! You were created to pass your passion for Jesus to the next generation. The shepherd's crook is ours, but only temporarily. We were born to make our ceiling the ground floor of the next generation.

When God speaks to you, it's always for a reason. His purpose is to increase your ability and confidence to do His will. Through vision, God confirms the granting of His authority and our boundaries as spiritual parents.

REVELATION AND SPIRITUAL AUTHORITY

Watchman Nee, in his book *Spiritual Authority*, taught, "Revelation is God's valuation and measurement. Authority is built on God's revelation, and His estimation of a person is according to that revelation. If God gives revelation, authority is established; but when His revelation is withdrawn, the man is rejected."[23]

God imparts vision to leaders He has chosen to accomplish His work on earth. We need to acknowledge and respect those God has placed in our midst to give visionary leadership. To do otherwise is to invite God's chastening. In Numbers 12, Aaron and Miriam challenged Moses, claiming that God had also spoken to them. Because of their presumption, the anger of the Lord burned against them. Miriam turned leprous and Aaron quickly pleaded for mercy. Occasionally those in subordinate positions will challenge the vision or authority of a senior leader. This may be for a variety of reasons. Perhaps they simply disagree. Or they may have an ulterior motive, like gathering followers to form a breakaway group.

Ultimately, God backs up those He has appointed to spiritual authority. Those who undermine God's leaders may appear to get what they want in the short term, but ultimately they face an uphill battle until they learn submission and a respect for authority. To challenge godly spiritual authority is no small matter to the Lord.

God's regard for earthly authority is found in Romans 13:1-2: "Everyone must submit himself to the governing authorities, for there is no authority except that which God has established. The authorities that exist have been established by God. Consequently, he who rebels against the authority is rebelling against what God has instituted, and those who do so will bring judgment on themselves."

These verses make it clear that it is God who establishes authorities. Even if we are required to serve under authorities that seem unreasonable or corrupt, God honors a submitted heart. To break Jacob of his cunning and cleverness, God required him to serve Laban, his unscrupulous father-in-law. It took fourteen years to bring Jacob to a point of release and blessing.

When our church was founded, God directed me to serve under a denominational covering that I often did not agree with. He promised that if I submitted to Him, in due time He would lift me up[24] and place me in the land where I belonged.

After seven painful years, God spoke to me in a dream and released me from my covering. He guided me step by step to ensure that the parting was amicable. As a result, the church was overwhelmingly united in the decision and we parted from our covering with a blessing.

KNOW YOUR BOUNDARY STONES

God gives vision to define our boundaries. The Lord has put boundary stones around our ministries. Just as Paul had limits to his apostolic authority, we must labor only within the fields where God has given us permission.

In biblical times, boundary stones were reference points that marked the extent of a person's property. Proverbs 23:10 says, "Do not move the ancient boundary stone, or encroach on the fields of the fatherless." A boundary stone was not to be moved. Why? To do so was to steal another man's land.

Even Jesus had boundaries. In John 5:19 He said, "I tell you the truth, the Son can do nothing by himself; he can do only what he sees his Father doing, because whatever the Father does the Son also does." For Jesus, His boundary was the will of the Father. Anything outside the Father's will was off-limits to the Son.

We receive numerous appeals to support the visions of other people and groups. As a pastor, I am often approached by people who want support for their projects or ministry. While we want to be generous, we must always ask, "What is God saying? Is this part of the vision the Lord has shown me? If I support this request, how will it affect my ability to accomplish what God is telling me to do?"

Have you ever heard the saying that something is so broad, it's shallow? When we move outside our boundary stones, we move out of God's grace and into the flesh. The results are predictable, we become ineffective and stressed. By trying to be all things to all people we usually end up satisfying no one.

WE CANNOT SIMPLY USE SOMEONE ELSE'S STRATEGY LIKE A MAGIC FORMULA!

This is one of the reasons that we cannot simply use someone else's strategy like a magic formula! Too often we chase after the successes of other leaders or fellowships. We think that if we just do what they have done, we will succeed! While we can learn from others, it will never be a substitute for seeking the Lord for ourselves. Remember, God wants to reveal His will directly to us.

THE POWER OF LOVE

Vision gives us an ability to see things clearly that were once obscure to us. For most of us, the single thing that has been most obscure is the importance of love. We are reminded in 1 Corinthians 13:13, "And now these three remain: faith, hope and love. But the greatest of these is love." What the body of Christ needs most is a fresh revelation of the power of love, and grace to live it out relationally.

To use the opening words of 1 Corinthians 13, we have taught people how to speak in tongues, to prophesy, to have faith, and give sacrificially. But unless we learn how to love, we remain lukewarm and devoid of passion, just like the Laodicean church. We need to heed the Spirit's word in Revelation 3:15–18:

> I know your deeds, that you are neither cold nor hot. I wish you were one or the other! So, because you are luke-warm—I am about to spit you out of my mouth. You say, "I am rich; I have acquired wealth and do not need a thing." But you do not realize that you are wretched, pitiful, poor, blind and naked. I counsel you to buy from me gold refined in the fire, so you can become rich; and white clothes to wear, so you can cover your shameful nakedness; and salve to put on your eyes, so you can see.

The Laodicean church suffered from self-satisfaction, distractions and passivity. Because they were blind to the importance of love, they needed eye surgery.

The "eye salve" we need is a revelation of love. This revelation comes in two ways: through vision and relationships. We need a vision of the power of love, but we also need relationships that teach us how love is lived out in everyday life. Love cannot be learned through a church program or course. We learn to love through the company we keep.

THE "EYE SALVE" WE NEED IS A REVELATION OF LOVE.

Remember 1 John 4:19, "We love because He first loved us." Our ability to love others is in direct proportion to the love of God we are regularly experiencing in our own lives. When was the last time you sensed the love of God for you?

We are called to love God first, and then our neighbor. We learn to love through relationships we have with other people, but particularly with other Christians. In Galatians 6:10 we are challenged, "Therefore, as we have opportunity, let us do good to all people, especially to those who belong to the family of believers."

Jesus wants us to be known as His disciples by the love we have for each other.[25]

Paul said in 1 Corinthians 13:11, "When I was a child, I talked like a child, I thought like a child, I reasoned like a child. When I became a man, I put childish ways behind me." Over the years I've watched sincere believers build theological foundations on faith or hope. While faith and hope are important, they are not the greatest.

For years, I tried to build the church on a leadership culture, signs and wonders, and the latest church growth strategies. While these things are not wrong, they are not God's best. Many times these things hide the real problem...a love deficit.

Without love, all of our strategies and programs will ultimately fail to produce a true legacy that can be passed from generation to generation. Only God can give grace to accomplish His will. He does this by revealing His love to us. His love empowers our love for others.

VISION AND PASSING ON YOUR BATON

One day I was listening to Harry Chapin's song, *The Cat's in the Cradle*. At the end of the chorus, the song goes, "And as I hung up the phone it occurred to me, he'd grown up just like me, my boy was just like me!" In that instant, God convicted me that I needed to be much more available as a spiritual father to my kids. They were in danger of turning out just like I did in my early life. That revelation stirred me to action.

Vision is God's blasting cap to propel you toward becoming a spiritual father or mother. Only when God reveals His heart will you be anointed with the passion, grace and perseverance necessary to give your life away. If you have not heard from Him, then continue to ask, seek and knock until He speaks. Draw near to God and He will draw near to you. Maybe it is time you slowed down long enough to hear from Him.

Since I've started making myself more available to others, I've had many moments of recognition. One minute you're sitting at the table with someone and in an instant God opens your eyes and you recognize Jesus in the person sitting next to you. We need to have more visions, more revelations, and more moments when God awakens in us the love he wants to pour through us to others.

For years, I struggled as a pastor to be all things to all people. My motives were not wrong, but my priorities were. I gave more time to the church than I did to relationships. I knew nothing about spiritual succession, a spirit of sonship or the importance of Malachi 4.

God revealed that if things didn't change soon, I would miss His highest purpose for my life, passing my baton on to the next generation.

The Lord is so kind. He loves His church and allowed me, like the prodigal son, to come to my senses. God birthed a vision in my heart. But vision is only the foundation of succession. The next step in our strategy is to learning to think and act in a way that enables succession.

Chapter Eight—Reality Check

- Has God revealed His heart for the next generation to you? Do you have a vision for passing on your baton to spiritual sons and daughters?

- Are you growing in your understanding of spiritual authority?

- When was the last time you experienced a sense of God's love for you? Given your gifting and personality, what are some ways you can express God's love to others?

CHAPTER NINE

PASSING ON THE BATON IN THE LOCAL CHURCH

But you will receive power when the Holy Spirit comes upon you; and you will be my witnesses in Jerusalem, and in Judea and Samaria, and to the ends of the earth.

—Acts 1:8

The men who followed Him were unique in their generation. They turned the world upside down because their hearts had been turned right side up. The world has never been the same. —Billy Graham

The purpose of the church is to fulfil God's two commands and the one commission. This means being committed to loving God, loving others and making disciples of all nations. Our effectiveness will be determined by the degree to which we are led by and surrendered to the Holy Spirit. Whatever our strategy for passing on the baton, it must be embraced and implemented first within the local church. We need to return to the only foundation worth building on—loving others as God loves us.

Bringing down the barriers

We are in a season where God is releasing His grace to see the generation gaps pulled down. If we are going to faithfully pass on our testimony of God's Word to the coming generations, we must put petty differences aside for the sake of love. It is time we model Jesus' ministry of reconciliation and reject gossip, slander and accusation.

Our spiritual sons and daughters need faithful followers of Christ to imitate, so that they too pass honor and blessing to their children. The first step in spiritual succession is recognizing the need for bringing down the barriers in relationships.

One day I was approached by a young man who confided that he was afraid of me. He went on to say that a number of his friends also thought I was intimidating and that they felt unable to approach me. For years I had been unaware that I was perceived as indifferent to the needs of young people. My silence in a number of situations had been misinterpreted as indifference. The young man's comment caused me to take stock of my life and how I come across.

How others perceive us has a direct bearing on our ability to build empowering relationships. Appearances and perceptions are extremely crucial. The judgments we make based on them can lead to problems if left unaddressed. While we cannot pander to every supposed hurt or insecurity in others, we need to be aware how others view us and do our best to dispel false perceptions.

One of the greatest barriers to spiritual succession in the local church is the division that comes from criticism and mistrust. The enemy is committed to sabotaging intergenerational relationships. He fears the power of a unified church where young and old work together in oneness of mind, spirit and purpose. Since his main weapon is deception, he tries to divide people by amplifying their differences.

Too often Christians are known more by their differences than they are for their love for one another! Differences can easily lead to misunderstandings that soon evolve into suspicion, gossip, slander and accusation. Before long, we end up playing a blame game of dishonor and hostility.

I have seen this intergenerational game played out several times in the body of Christ, with devastating consequences. Frustrated young people complain that older people don't trust them and don't want to understand them. Older folk complain about the impatience of young people.

And then there's the social labelling. Busters get angry with Baby Boomers and blame them for missed leadership opportunities and over-the-top materialism. Generation X accuses their leaders of having a control spirit and taking aeons to do anything. Then the Baby Boomers complain about Generation Y not having respect for authority. The Establishers wonder why we don't do things the same way anymore and complain that the music is way too loud!

If all this carry-on wasn't so serious it would be funny! But it is serious, and it leads to division and fractured relationships. Galatians 5:15 warns us that if we keep on biting and devouring each other we will end up being destroyed by each other.

Remember the blame game between David and Absalom?[26] Following the injustice of his half-sister's rape by Amnon, his half-brother, Absalom retaliated by having him murdered. Fearing the anger of his father, Absalom fled to Geshur, where he lived in exile for three years.

Under pressure, King David eventually sent for Absalom, but then held him at a distance. David's apparent indifference toward his son resulted in such bitterness that Absalom began to undermine his father's authority and eventually usurped his kingdom.

If the truth be known, David was not really indifferent to his son, but he appeared to be indifferent. Why? David refused to see Absalom and spend time restoring relationship with his son. His silence and lack of action resulted in a bitter root for the enemy to manipulate.

Bitterness feeds an *independent* spirit that is rife in the church today. This spirit or attitude focuses on the importance of the individual. Individualism is a worldly philosophy that promotes self-interest and a culture of self. Whenever we hear Christians regularly using terminology like, my spiritual gift, my ministry, my vision and "God is the only one I submit to," it reflects the influence of individualism on our thinking.

Ultimately, individualism lies at the root of an *orphan spirit.* Remember the orphan spirit stands in direct contrast to a spirit of sonship. It exhibits a fierce independence to protect itself and results in a pride that undermines unity in the body of Christ. It spawns leaders who focus on empire-building rather than body building. Lack of relationship and mentoring has produced too many enclaves of angry, independent men and women who have been seduced by Satan's blame game.

Rather than an unhealthy independence, God's desire is dependence on Him and interdependence with each other. In 1 John 3:16 we read, "This is how we know what love is: Jesus Christ laid down his life for us. And we ought to lay down our lives for our brothers."

The heart of passing on the baton is laying down our lives for others. It is doing everything in our power to help others grow in Christ. The enemy wants to divide us so our love for one another goes cold. This will render us ineffective. Only love, shown in tangible ways, can disarm blame and defeat individualism.

DEPENDING ON GOD

Just to make it clear, there is no single method or sure-fire formula for spiritual succession. We have to depend on God. The only thing we have worth passing on originated with Him to begin with. This is why we need God's grace. Anything else will be based on the flesh and will inevitably lead our sons and daughters right back to institutional thinking and superficial relationships.

We have to depend on God as we identify, train, and release sons and daughters.

Remember the importance of properly identifying our spiritual sons and daughters. In chapter six we discovered this means choosing the right people to build into. I remember an old Iowa proverb that says, "It's much easier to ride a horse in the direction it's already going!" We cannot successfully build into men and women who have not been given to us by the Lord. The Lord knows who will bear fruit and who will not. He wants to link us with people of His choosing.

Trust God to show you the men and women who are potential sons and daughters. Make a list of them. Ask the Holy Spirit for grace and wisdom in your choices. Expect God to speak to you clearly concerning whether you should approach them or they should approach you. Is the timing right? Test your inner registrations. Ask God for clear confirmation. He wants you to link with the right people, those He chooses. He wants to answer your prayer.

Once we have chosen a man or woman to build into, parenting involves a dimension of training. Notice I said *a* dimension. This means that we can't train them in every area, only where we ourselves have been graced. The best plan is to look at the way Jesus trained.

First, He modeled what he wanted to teach and the disciples watched Him. Next, the disciples did what Jesus modeled and He observed and corrected them. Then, Jesus' disciples went on out in pairs to practise, and reported back to Him. Finally, they repeated the process with others, thus reproducing themselves.

A good spiritual father or mother is aware of their God-given limits, or *boundaries of grace*. God has designed us to be interdependent. None of us can do all things well, but we can all do some things well. If we operate within the grace God has given, we will be more effective, fulfilled and able to empower others.

As we seek to empower others, we are wise to ask, "Father, what are you doing in this person's life? How can I best build into them? What can I do that will cooperate with your will in this person's life?" To see Christ formed in our sons and daughters requires that others see Jesus in our lives.

The Commission

In Acts 1:8, Jesus laid out His strategy for kingdom expansion: "You will be my witnesses in Jerusalem, and in Judea and Samaria, and to the ends of the earth." This was a simple plan; easy to remember. Like a ripple effect, Jesus saw succession as a progression from local to regional and finally to international.

Jesus was, in effect, saying, *Tell everyone about me. Bring them into relationship with my Father. Love each other deeply. Begin building empowering relationships locally in Jerusalem. As the church in Jerusalem is established, you will then have teams who are able and confident to go to the nearby regions of Judea and Samaria. As they respond to the good news about me, momentum will increase. Soon, you will have a team, filled with grace, who will be my witnesses to the ends of the earth.*

This raises an important question. How then does Jesus' Commission translate into a local church setting?

Our plan for spiritual succession often comes from a mission statement. For our mission statement at Churchlands, we have embraced Jesus' two commands and the Great Commission. These three directives are simple, easily remembered and provide a great template for plotting and evaluating our course.

These priorities keep love and relationships at the top of our agenda. Loving God with all our heart, loving our neighbors as ourselves, and making disciples out of all the nations—these provide a compass heading for the entire church.

The outworking of this mission statement gives rise to a simple strategy we call 3-3-3.

	1	2	3
Our Mission	Love God	Love each other	Make disciples of all nations
Our Priorities	Transform the local church	Raise up the five-fold ministries	Send workers into the harvest fields
Our Strategy	Link spiritual mothers and fathers to sons and daughters	Raise up a church within a church	Mobilize local and trans-local mission teams

Our goal in the 3-3-3 strategy is to raise a church within a church. We are developing a team of emerging young leaders, spiritual sons and daughters, in the midst of our existing leadership team. Our goal is to gradually hand over leadership now rather than wait till the current team retires. This process also enables current leaders to function as spiritual fathers and mothers to the emerging team.

Within our local church setting, we have targeted two areas where young leaders can be raised up within existing programs: the café and the worship ministry. This enables emerging leaders to learn the value of teamwork, develop serving skills, and have opportunities to shape the content and style of our services. Relationships between generations are galvanized through practical, hands-on ways of working together.

While strategy is important, sometimes the best thing you can do as a spiritual parent is go with the Spirit's flow and be flexible. While we have a strategy for succession in our local fellowship, we are prepared to change it if God reveals a better way.

In establishing a culture of passing on the baton in your local church I'd like to leave you with a few suggestions.

- Withstand the temptation to introduce major change too quickly. Evolutionary change is better than revolutionary.

- Consider how passing on the baton arises from your mission statement. The best mission statements are scriptural, reflect the heart of Jesus, and are easily remembered.

- Think of spiritual succession in terms of concentric circles. Begin locally and plan for expansion.

- Beware of the enemy's wiles when you try to build bridges between generations, particularly the blame game.

- Depend on God. It is the key to passing on your baton successfully.

- Stay humble. Be a good listener, remain soft, and above all, be yourself. Attitude is everything in spiritual parenting.

In the next chapter, we see how passing on the baton results in the formation and release of the five-fold ministry.

CHAPTER NINE—REALITY CHECK

- Have you ever been caught up in an intergenerational blame game? Are you holding any wrong attitudes toward persons older or younger than yourself?

- What are the boundaries of your grace? What can you impart to others as a result of your experiences and gifts?

- How can you encourage others to pass on their baton within your local church?

CHAPTER TEN

RESTORING THE
FIVE-FOLD MINISTRY

It was he (Jesus) who gave some to be apostles, some to be prophets, some to be evangelists, and some to be pastors and teachers, to prepare God's people for works of service, so that the body of Christ may be built up until we all reach unity in the faith and in the knowledge of the Son of God and become mature, attaining to the whole measure of the fullness of Christ.

—Ephesians 4:11–13

Team work makes the dream work.

—John Maxwell

We often think of the five ministries equipping the saints largely in terms of ministry gifts or abilities. The real significance of the five-fold ministries in the church today lies not only in their gifting but in the character and love of Christ they bring in restoring the church to its true foundations. While skills are important, the major task of these ministries is threefold: to form and release individuals and teams into apostolic teams, to be spiritual fathers and mothers, and to keep the church on a relational foundation.

In many parts of the church, there seems to be a sense of mystery and nostalgia that hangs over the five-fold ministries of Ephesians 4. To some church leaders, the thought of apostles and prophets in the twenty-first century is an unachievable myth. Others, however, see them like the Jedi Knights in Star Wars, hoping they will someday return to restore order and stability to the universe. Such is the polarity of views on the subject.

While some church leaders embrace a dispensational view that the five-fold ministries have disappeared and are a spent force, others disagree. My belief is that these equippers of the saints will return to take their place in preparing the church for Christ's return.

That controversy would surround the five-fold ministries of Ephesians 4 should not come as any great surprise. The enemy has a vested interest in keeping the church in a state of disarray. Whether we are for or against the concept of modern day apostles, prophets, evangelists, pastors and teachers is a moot point. The wise course is to heed the advice of Gamaliel and let God have the final say.

THE APOSTOLIC VISION

The Greek word *apostolos* means "one who is sent." The early apostles fulfilled a unique and foundational role in establishing the early church and taking the gospel to the ends of the earth. Following the deaths of the original twelve apostles, the apostolic line continued as the church recognized the character, gifting and call on anointed men and women.

As time progressed and Christianity became more established and socially accepted, the church evolved structurally to accommodate the needs of a large membership and the increasingly influential role it played in government and society. What was once the role of the five-fold ministries in church leadership, teaching, and equipping God's people evolved into an ecclesiastical system ruled by bishops, priests and monastics.

The sheer numbers of people who now embraced the Christian faith made it almost impossible for clergy to empower the rank and file within their congregations. Rather than equipping the entire people of God, the *layos*, their attention turned toward training only professional clergy, the *cleros*.

Christianity gradually devolved from a grass roots movement to one dominated by professional priests. Following the fall of the Roman Empire and during the ensuing dark ages, the clergy became the most influential teachers in the western world. In most communities, priests were about the only people who were able to read and write. This contributed to a widening of the gap between church leaders and the average person.

Not until the Protestant reformation of the 16th century, and the rediscovery of the concept of the priesthood of all believers, did this gap begin to close. Since that time, every season and message of reform has enabled the church to rediscover and reclaim a body of spiritual truth that had been lost for centuries.

The Lord is now highlighting yet another body of truth that has been lost: the significance of the five-fold ministries of New Testament apostles, prophets, evangelists, pastors and teachers. While the church has embraced pastors, teachers and evangelists for centuries, only in recent decades have the ministries of prophets and apostles received widespread attention. This is significant, because the fulfillment of Malachi 4:5–6 cannot take place without prophetic and apostolic ministries in place.

WISDOM AND REVELATION

Apostles and prophets carry an anointing to release greater wisdom and revelation within the church. The apostolic and prophetic are designed by God to balance and complement each other. As justice balances mercy and truth balances grace, so apostles and prophets combine wisdom and revelation in a way that releases God's people in ministry.

So what do God's wisdom and revelation reveal concerning Malachi 4:5–6? These verses speak of Elijah coming. He represents the true prophets of the Lord. Elijah was also a spiritual father who faithfully passed his mantle to Elisha.

The revelation God is bringing to the church through His prophets is that there are relational barriers between the generations. In this season of grace, the words of the prophets carry a transformational power to pull down barriers and usher in a new wineskin—a more relational church where the hearts of the older and younger generations turn toward each other.

Apostolic wisdom teaches us how best to apply this revelation. The hearts of the generations can only be united if they are knit together in the love of Christ. We need God's perspective to determine *how* and *where* to build relationships that empower others. I believe this is one of the reasons that modern day apostles are emerging.

Apostles represent the fatherhood of God over the church. Wherever true apostles go, they bring a relational anointing and the wisdom of God to build up the church in love, unity and mutual respect. Like our heavenly Father, apostles are jealous to see God's people in right relationship with Him, bonded in love with each other and walking in Christ.

When apostles minister with prophets, an even greater dimension of wisdom and revelation is released. This dimension is crucial for generations to pass on their baton successfully to the next. As the ministry of apostles and prophets joins with the other five-fold ministries of evangelists, pastors and teachers, a synergy will occur that releases teams capable of functioning in a realm far wider than the local church. The purpose of apostolic ministry teams is to reproduce and proliferate themselves throughout the body of Christ.

Gifts to the Church

The Greek word for "gifts" we find in Ephesians 4:8, *doma*, implies the "gift of a person," in contrast to the "gift of an anointing," or *charis*, mentioned in Paul's description of spiritual gifts in 1 Corinthians 12. Consequently, the five-fold ministries are **gifts of people** given to the church by the ascended Christ, to continue His ministry of equipping and releasing.

Each five-fold ministry person embodies a facet of Jesus' ministry that He has left on earth to build up His church. When all five ministries function cooperatively, they establish the church in the fullness of Christ's gifts and character.

The five-fold anointing is powerful because the character of Christ and the death of self are so evident in these men and women. The five-fold ministries are able to increase the effectiveness of the church because of the death of their flesh.

True equippers are not enamored with their gift, skills or abilities. They do not find their identity in what they do, and so do not seek praise from men. Instead, their identity is found in Christ. They want to reflect the incredible depth of God's love and grace, and desire to see all God's people bonded in this love.

In the coming days, we will see a shift in how the five-fold ministry is viewed. Too often, God's people have put these "sent ones" on a pedestal, idolizing them for their gift or God's power at work through them. We need to recognize these equippers for who they are: gifts to the body of Christ but also fellow servants. Their goal is that the church be built up in love, unity, and knowing Jesus. Only then can the church fulfil the Great Commission.

Releasing the Five-Fold Ministries

Realizing how crucial this would be in the coming years, at Churchlands we set out to develop a model to identify, train and release the five-fold ministries. Following Acts 1:8, we have designed a three-phase pilot project to build up equippers of the saints.

Our first step was to invite twenty people to participate. Our group was made up of five people who had prophetic gifting, five who were teachers, five with pastoral gifts and five evangelists. We did not select anyone with apostolic gifting because we believe that apostles gradually arise from the other four.

The plan for the first phase was to ask each participant to commit to four personal disciplines.

- Participate in a monthly meeting of the entire group to receive teaching on five-fold related topics, discuss our progress, and break into small groups for discussion.

- Meet monthly with a team facilitator and assume the role of son or daughter to a spiritual father or mother.

- Participate in selected conferences and read six books relevant to our preparation for five-fold ministry.

- Partner with another member of the group to engage in spontaneous, hands-on ministry as opportunities presented themselves during the week.

Our goal in the four activities was to provide just enough structure to stretch everyone's perspectives on five-fold ministry. Believing that apostolic ministry is a team activity, we knew that the team players would eventually surface. Knowing that the five-fold arises from spiritual sons and daughters, we soon discovered those who sought relationship more than just a platform to advance their ministries.

In the second phase, we introduced the concept of apprenticeship and exposed the group to people having gifts different from their own. It is interesting to watch the creative tension between pastors, evangelists, teachers and prophets as they learn to appreciate and interact with one another.

In the third phase, we decreased the frequency of large group meetings, moving from monthly to quarterly. We encouraged each team member to link with spiritual fathers and mothers in Paul and

Timothy types of relationship, meeting regularly, travelling together on mission trips and learning to minister within a team.

To use the analogy of concentric circles, the purpose of the first phase is to gather people into an inner circle experience, relatively structured, and giving maximum exposure to the principles of five-fold ministry. The second phase introduces the concept of apprenticeship and learning by doing. The third phase introduces the group to the journeyman model.

The goal of the five-fold ministry is to multiply and to enable spiritual succession. The progression from apprentice to journeyman to craftsman is the pattern we observe in the ministry of Jesus. As apostles, prophets, evangelists, pastors and teachers are sent forth as teams, the ministry of Jesus is established and multiplied on the earth.

TOWARD A CULTURE OF EQUIPPING

The five-fold are, by definition, those who impart their abilities to others and equip the saints for the work of ministry. They know when it is best to speak as a mentor, coach, sponsor, or simply to be an example. They understand the progression of spiritual growth from apprentice to journeyman to craftsman because they have been through it themselves. They are catalysts toward establishing a culture of honor and succession.

Relationship is the basis of trust. As we have seen, passing on the baton cannot take place outside of relationship. When we pass on a legacy to our successors, we do more than simply give information or possessions, we give our lives. Our legacy is our life. It is easier to give of our life to another person, and for them to receive what we give, if we have an established level of trust and confidence in that person.

OUR LEGACY IS OUR LIFE.

Because the five-fold ministries are mobile and move from place to place, they are well positioned to fan the flame of spiritual succession across the globe. Their nature is to gravitate toward establishing on-going relationships that have the potential to bear lasting fruit.

One of the great insights to come out of Promise Keepers is that every person needs three people in their lives: a Paul, a Barnabas, and a Timothy. A Paul figure is someone who we look up to and, while they are not a close friend, we are inspired to follow them as they follow Christ.[27] Barnabas is someone whom we give permission to encourage us and to speak honestly into our lives on an ongoing basis. Timothy is a younger person into whose life we are building as a spiritual son or daughter.

A pertinent question for us all is, "Do we have these three types of people in our lives?" We all need models, encouragers and protégés if we are to grow into the full stature of Christ. The five-fold ministries make local leaders accountable to making sure that everyone has someone they are investing in for the future. This accountability and support are essential to establishing a culture of succession within the body of Christ.

In the next chapter, we see the inevitable result of raising and releasing the five-fold ministries: the emergence of Antioch churches.

CHAPTER TEN—REALITY CHECK

- What is your view of the significance of the five-fold ministry gifts in Ephesians 4 in the church today?

- Who are the Paul, Barnabas and Timothy figures in your life?

- Reflect on the apprentice, journeyman, craftsman model for developing the five-fold ministries within a local congregation. Consider developing a plan that would utilize the gifts of people within your own church.

CHAPTER ELEVEN

DEVELOPING AN ANTIOCH PERSPECTIVE

In the church at Antioch there were prophets and teachers: Barnabas, Simeon called Niger, Lucius of Cyrene, Manaen (who had been brought up with Herod the Tetrarch) and Saul. While they were worshiping the Lord and fasting, the Holy Spirit said, "Set apart for me Barnabas and Saul for the work to which I have called them." So after they had fasted and prayed, they placed their hands on them and sent them off. —Acts 13:1–3

If a man is interested in himself only, he is very small; if he is interested in his family, he is larger; if he is interested in his community, he is larger still. —Aristotle

For too long, local churches have delegated the responsibility of fulfilling the Great Commission to mission and para-church organizations. Antioch was a sending church, with a vision far beyond their city and region. They released Barnabas and Saul to take the gospel to the ends of the earth. The ultimate goal of spiritual succession is raising Antioch-type churches. These have a vi-

sion for sending empowered men and women into the world who can multiply themselves and make disciples of all the nations.

I once heard a well-known Christian leader lament, "One of the greatest frustrations in ministry is not knowing whether you are kicking any goals." In sport, it's easy to know if you're succeeding; you are scoring goals. The scoreboard gives you an immediate indication of whether you're winning or losing.

JESUS NEVER USED THE WORD *SUCCESS*. HE DID, HOWEVER, SPEAK OF *FAITHFULNESS*.

Ministry, however, is different. How do we measure progress and know if we are successful? Is it Sunday church attendance? Is it the size of our church budget? Is it the number of decisions for Christ? How many books we've written? Is it our reputation?

Jesus never used the word *success*. He did, however, speak of *faithfulness*. To God, our faithfulness is much more important than success. He made this clear in the parable of the talents. In Matthew 25:21, we note that the steward who brought a good return on the master's investment was commended for his positive attitude and his wise actions: "Well done, good and faithful servant! You have been faithful with a few things; I will put you in charge of many things. Come and share your master's happiness!"

Faithfulness is measured in attitude and proven in actions. Actions produce results which people often label as success, but God also sees the heart.[28] Someday each of us will stand before God to give account of how we have invested the talents He gave to us. God is the owner of all talents; we are temporary stewards and managers of His resources.

As the pastor of a large church, the proper use of resources is always very close to my heart. I want to see sons and daughters who become spiritual fathers and mothers. I want to see five-fold ministers raised and released and see our ministry do all it can to advance God's kingdom and become an Antioch church.

THE PROPHECY OF SHIPS

My thinking was challenged when our church hosted a ministry conference featuring well-known prophetic author Rick Joyner. On the final day of the conference, Rick shared a vision God had given him regarding Churchlands and the city of Perth. In the vision he saw many ships going back and forth between Australia and Africa. Some of the ships were troop ships and others were cargo ships. This vision spoke to me concerning the future.

For several years, I have been ministering regularly in churches in southern Africa. About ten years ago, I sensed God stirring me to establish a relational network that would link ministries throughout the Southern Hemisphere. This network would build supportive friendships between Christian leaders, with strong bridges built between Australia and Africa.

When Rick spoke this prophetic word, I was jolted into a new understanding of God's purposes. The cargo ships represented His Holy Spirit being poured out on the nations to fulfil the Great Commission. The troop ships were thousands of young people who were about to be mobilized and travel to the nations. I could see that our bridge building between nations was part of this. Preparations had to be made.

The Lord showed me a connection between sending ships and the church in Antioch. The Antioch Church released many apostolic teams. God's ultimate plan is to raise up many Antiochs, many sending churches in unity in their cities, who will equip and send apostolic teams in the days to come.

THE ANTIOCH MODEL

While several early churches are mentioned as having prominence in the New Testament, three stand out: Jerusalem, Antioch and Ephesus. We can see in these three churches a progression of how the early church developed. Jerusalem was the mother church in the sense of being where Christianity began. The dynamics of relational life in the Jerusalem church are spelled out in Acts 2:42–45 and 4:32–35. It was a caring church that sent equippers like Barnabas and Agabus to Antioch[29] to build up the wider body.

As Antioch and other second generation churches grew, more teams were sent to build up fledgling churches. Paul and Barnabas were sent from Antioch.[30]

It appears that the strategy of brief apostolic visits to fledgling churches was not as effective as longer term relationships with strategic churches. Therefore, on his third missionary journey, we see Paul remaining for three years in the church of Ephesus. From an *itinerant* model, the five-fold ministries came to *reside* in strategic churches and engaged in training and sending teams into the harvest field.

Antioch was a port city located on the eastern edge of the Mediterranean; it was a thriving center of commerce. It was also home to people from a vast array of nations and cultures. This made Antioch a perfect location for a sending church.

While its location was important, it had a dynamic of spiritual life that made it outward looking and effective in releasing leaders to the harvest field. Colossians 1:3–8 gives us a clue as to what Paul considered to be the attributes of a healthy church.

> We always thank God, the Father of our Lord Jesus Christ, when we pray for you, because we have heard of your faith in Christ Jesus and of the love you have for all the saints—the faith and love that spring from the hope that is stored up for you in heaven and that you have already heard about in the word of truth, the gospel that has come to you. All over the world this gospel is bearing fruit and growing, just as it has been doing among you since the day you heard it and understood God's grace in all its truth. You learned it from Epaphras, our dear fellow servant, who is a faithful minister of Christ on our behalf, and who also told us of your love in the Spirit.

The church at Colosse was commended for seven qualities:

- Faith in Christ Jesus (v 4)
- Love for all the saints (v 4)
- Faith and love that spring from hope (v 5)
- Hearing the word of truth, the gospel (v 5)
- The gospel bearing fruit (v 6)
- An understanding of God's grace (v 6)
- Learning from Epaphras, a spiritual father (v 7)

Healthy, outward-looking churches are committed to the mandate of the two commands and one Great Commission. They are committed to hearing the word of truth. They are bearing fruit and growing in their understanding of God's grace. And finally, they receive the ministry of spiritual fathers.

Today we need more churches like Colosse and Antioch who have a vision for sending. These are the churches who, like Antioch, will launch ships and mobilize coming generations to fulfil the Great Commission.

A VISION FOR SENDING

I believe God's strategy for launching ships has four stages. The first stage is to invigorate life and relationships within the local church. God sees the local congregation as the best place to raise spiritual sons and daughters. For this to happen, the hearts of fathers and mothers must be turned to the children. Then a spirit of sonship will begin to emerge and a culture of honor develop.

Second, out of a culture of relationship and honor the five-fold equipping ministries of Ephesians 4 will arise. These ministries, because of the grace and abilities they carry, become leaders of apostolic teams who equip the saints for works of service. But equipping is not their only focus; they also bring unity, knowledge of the Son of God, and have a heart to see Christlike character established within the saints.

As sons and daughters are equipped by the five-fold, they can then be released into service. In this third stage, teams of young and seasoned Christians are sent from churches with an Antioch vision. These churches will launch troop ships and cargo ships filled with enthusiastic and gifted men and women with a vision of the harvest.

Finally, not all of the ships will return home full of passengers. Some who have left their homes will remain with the people they have chosen to serve. Like Paul, who spent three years in Ephesus, these men and women will equip indigenous peoples to raise workers *for* the harvest *from* the harvest.

Antioch was the first place where people were actually called Christians. Something about these people so reflected the heart and passion of Jesus that the world sat up and took notice. Billy Graham once said, "The men who followed Him were unique in their generation. They turned the world upside down because their hearts had been turned right side up. The world has never been the same."

In this day, God is calling the church to faithfulness and to raise and release men and women who will expand the boundaries of His kingdom. The goal of spiritual succession is more than raising spiritual sons and daughters, more than releasing the five-fold. The goal is to take the gospel to the ends of the earth!

CHAPTER ELEVEN—REALITY CHECK

- In ministry, is your focus on success or faithfulness?

- How does your local church measure up to the seven qualities of the church at Colosse?

- What can you do to encourage a culture of sending within your local church?

CHAPTER TWELVE

EVERY JOURNEY BEGINS...

God is love. Whoever lives in love lives in God, and God in him. In this way, love is made complete among us so that we will have confidence on the day of judgment, because in this world we are like him.

—1 John 4:16–17

I used to ask God to help me. Then I asked if I might help Him. I ended up by asking Him to do His work through me.

—Hudson Taylor

Every journey begins with a single step. The future of the body of Christ depends on returning to the relational roots of the early church. God is calling His people back to the pre-eminence of His love.

Several years ago I listened to a sermon by the late pastor Brent Rue that changed my heart and the way I view others. The message, based on 1 John 4:19, was called, "Letting God Love You." Brent's premise was that we can love others only to the extent that we have personally experienced God's love for us.

"DURING YOUR LIFE ON EARTH, DID YOU LEARN HOW TO LOVE?"

We cannot love others out of a sense of compulsion or duty; love arises from a sense of gratitude of having personally experienced God's love. The more of God's love we have experienced, the more we can truly love others!

Brent concluded his message with a picture of heaven that God gave to him in a dream. On Judgment Day, each of us will stand before the Lord and He will ask us only one simple question, "During your life on earth, did you learn how to love?"

What God wants of us is not more programs, more performances or more sacrifices. He wants our hearts and for us to love others in the same way He has loved us. Malachi 4:5–6 calls us to emulate the Father's love by rearranging our priorities and turning our hearts to those who will come after us in the continuum of history.

I can't think of anything more exciting, or impossible, than seeing the entire church committed to relationships that genuinely empower and release young, inexperienced men and women into service. In fact, the odds are so heavily stacked against such radical change that only God can do it!

YOUR MOMENT HAS COME

The majority of movers and shakers in God's kingdom have always been ordinary people. The people who will ultimately fulfil the prophecy of Malachi 4:5–6 are average men and women who, for the most part, are not well known beyond their local community. These are the people who will bridge the gap between generations and see the church return to its relational foundations.

As spiritual fathers and mothers build into sons and daughters, a new church culture will rise. This culture will reflect the fullness of the ministry of Jesus. It will be based on honor and mutual submission. It will reflect the loving unity of the Father, Son and Holy Spirit.

Love bears its most lasting fruit through one-on-one, empowering relationships. Showing love in this way will return the hearts of the children to the fathers. Consider for a moment, if you have progressed in life it is because *someone* cared enough to encourage and empower you.

Charles L. Allen once wrote,

No member of God's team trains for the race without one day being given a chance to run. Sooner or later God says to every person who is ready, "Now—now, your moment has come."[31]

Every journey begins with a single step. We have not truly finished the race of faith until we have passed the baton to the next generation. The time has come to be courageous, face our fears, and make ourselves available to others. We have all been given a mantle, a baton, a shepherd's crook, *but it's not ours to keep!*

The moment has come for all of us, young and old, to run the race and pass the baton of God's Word to our sons and daughters. The church can no longer sit idly by while our youth are seduced by the world and its values. The only way forward is the way of Christ's love; a love that makes our ceiling the ground floor of the next generation.

Love

John

EXTRA MATERIAL

This is the complete table of the differences between sons and orphans by Chuck Clayton. The abbreviated version can be found in chapter six.

The Heart of a Son	The Heart of an Orphan
Sons build the house.	Orphans serve in the house out of duty, doing only what they have to.
Sons hold the father's vision as their own and seek to accomplish it.	Orphans serve only the parts of the vision that they like.
Sons speak by using family language: we—our—us—one another.	Orphans use individual terminology: me—my—I—mine.
Sons are family-oriented.	Orphans are issue-oriented— being right is most important (so they will split over issues).
Sons will submit to the father's authority.	Orphans frequently question decisions.
Sons will build into the lives of others and want to pass on their baton to others.	Orphans keep people dependent on them and will not pass on their baton to others.

Sons bond newcomers into the family.	Orphans gather new people to themselves.
Sons focus on serving and the well-being of the people.	Orphans focus on appearances and how to look good.
Sons are transparent—they share their inner thoughts and feelings.	Orphans share only what they want you to know.
Sons are secure and will receive correction.	Orphans become defensive when corrected. They see correction as rejection and blame others.
Sons start awkwardly in spiritual things, but gradually mature in them.	Orphans will not step out or take chances, because they fear failure.
Sons are hopeful and expectant of the future.	Orphans would rather focus on the past.
Sons are more concerned about relationships.	Orphans are concerned about rules and regulations.
Sons have a stake in the family business, knowing they have an inheritance.	Orphans look for sundown and a paycheck.
Sons stay put under fire.	Orphans look for greener pastures.

ENDNOTES

CHAPTER ONE: THINGS HAVE GOT TO CHANGE!

1   Malachi 4:5–6 (NIV)

CHAPTER TWO: LEAVING A LEGACY

2   John Maxwell, *The 21 Irrefutable Laws of Leadership* (Nashville: Thomas Nelson Publishers, 1998), p. 221.

3   Colin Noyes, *The Coaching Process*, CoachNet Pacific. Colin Noyes is the Australian director of CoachNet Pacific.

CHAPTER THREE: THE CHURCH'S DILEMMA

4   Graham McRobb, "Parable of the Surf-lifesaving Club," *Friendship Evangelism*, Adult Christian Education Foundation, Chullora, NSW, Australia.

5   Matthew 13:1–23 (NIV)

6   James 4:8

CHAPTER FOUR: BRIDGING THE GAP

7   Proverbs 13:22

8   John Maxwell, *The 21 Irrefutable Laws of Leadership* (Nashville: Thomas Nelson Publishers, 1998).

9   Hattaway, Paul, *The Heavenly Man: The Remarkable True Story of Chinese Christian Brother Yun,* London: Monarch Books, 2002.

10   1 Thessalonians 2:8

Chapter Five: Building a Culture of Honor

11   John 13:34–35

12   Deuteronomy 5:16

Chapter Six: Growing in a Spirit of Sonship

13   Matthew 25:21

14   John 5:19–20

15   Clayton, Chuck. *Slaves Versus Sons,* Chuck is an apostolic leader and overseer of Antioch Ministries, Indiana, USA.

16   Bill Hybels, *Courageous Leadership*, Grand Rapids, Zondervan, 2002, pp 80–85.

17   1 Samuel 16:7

Chapter Seven: Becoming a Spiritual Parent

18   Colin Noyes, *The Coaching Process*, CoachNet Pacific. Colin Noyes is the Australian director of CoachNet Pacific.

19   Matthew 10:16

20   2 Timothy 1:13

Chapter Eight: A Change of Heart

21   Acts 9

22   Luke 24:32

23 Watchman Nee, *Spiritual Authority*, New York, Christian Fellowship Publishers, 1972, p. 129.

24 1 Peter 5:6

25 John 13:35

CHAPTER NINE: SUCCESSION IN THE LOCAL CHURCH

26 2 Samuel 13–15

CHAPTER TEN: RESTORING THE FIVE-FOLD MINISTRY

27 1 Corinthians 4:15–16

CHAPTER ELEVEN: DEVELOPING AN ANTIOCH PERSPECTIVE

28 1 Samuel 16:7

29 Acts 11:22, 27–28

30 Acts 13:1–3

CHAPTER TWELVE: EVERY JOURNEY BEGINS...

31 Charles L Allen, "Service" in *Wings of Joy,* compiled and edited by Joan Winmill Brown, Old Tappan, New Jersey, Fleming H. Revell Company, 1977, p. 88.